Learn SQL: A Beginner's Guid[...] Database Basics with[...]

By Liam Doherty

Contents

Welcome to SQL: Your First Step into Databases

Hello there, and a hearty welcome to the world of SQL! You're about to embark on a journey into databases, and I'm genuinely excited to walk you through it, step by gentle step. My name's Liam Doherty, a coder hailing from the windswept shores of Galway, Ireland, where I've spent years helping folks just like you— beginners with a spark of curiosity—get comfortable with technology. SQL, or Structured Query Language if we're being formal, is your ticket to managing and making sense of data. It's a language that's both simple to grasp and incredibly powerful, used by everyone from small startups to global giants. Whether you're dreaming of organizing your personal projects, sifting through numbers for insights, or just picking up a skill to dazzle your friends over a pint, this book is here to guide you with clarity and care. Let's ease into it together, build your confidence, and get you working with data in ways you'll be proud of—sound good?

So, what's SQL all about? Imagine databases as those big, orderly filing cabinets you might find in an old library, stuffed with information waiting to be explored. SQL is the language you use to talk to them—to ask questions like "Can you show me all the customers from Dublin?" or "How many books did I lend out last month?" It's the backbone of how data gets handled in the modern world. Big companies like Amazon use SQL to keep track of millions of products in their warehouses, hospitals rely on it to manage patient records down to the last detail, and even the apps on your phone—like the one you use to order takeaway—depend on it to fetch your favorite curry order from their servers. It's versatile, it's free to learn, and it works on any computer you've got, whether it's a creaky old Windows laptop, a shiny Mac, or that Linux machine your techie cousin swore by.

What makes SQL special is how approachable it is. The commands you'll learn—like SELECT, INSERT, or WHERE—read almost like plain English, so you won't feel like you're deciphering some ancient code. It's designed to be intuitive, letting you focus on what you want to do with your data rather than wrestling with complicated syntax. And here's the best part: you're not alone on this journey. There's a massive community of SQL users out there—thousands of folks sharing tips, answering questions, and posting solutions online. If you ever hit a snag, a quick search will light the way forward. I've written this book with you, the absolute beginner, in mind. We'll assume you've never touched a database before, and we'll start from the ground up. No jargon, no rush—just the essentials, explained clearly, with plenty of examples to try out. By the end, you'll be building practical little tools with SQL, all at a pace that feels just right.

Think of this as a friendly chat over a cup of tea. We'll cover how to set up your tools, create your own databases, ask questions of your data, and even fix mistakes when they pop up. You'll see how SQL can help with real-life tasks—like tracking your weekly shopping list, managing a book club's reading schedule, or keeping tabs on birthdays you don't want to forget. All you need to bring is a computer (any kind will do) and a bit of willingness to explore. SQL's got the rest covered, and I'll be right here with you, breaking it down into bite-sized pieces. Picture yourself a few chapters from now, confidently pulling data out of a table you built yourself, maybe even showing it off to a friend— "Look what I made!" That's where we're headed, and I can't wait to see you get there. So, let's turn the page and get started—your adventure with SQL begins now!

Getting Started: Setting Up SQL on Your Computer

Right, let's roll up our sleeves and get SQL running on your machine—it's a lot simpler than you might imagine, and I'll walk you through every bit of it. We're going to use SQLite, a lightweight database system that's perfect for beginners like you. It doesn't need a big, complicated server setup, and it's free as the wind blowing across Galway Bay. First stop: head over to sqlite.org, the official home of SQLite. Once you're there, look for the "Download" section—it's usually right near the top. You'll want the latest version available as of April 2025, which should be something like SQLite 3.45. Don't worry if the number's a tad different; anything recent will do just fine.

If you're on Windows, scroll down to the "Precompiled Binaries for Windows" section and grab the "sqlite-tools-win32-x86" zip file—it's a small package with everything you need. Download it, then unzip it into a folder you'll remember, like "C:\SQLite." Inside, you'll find "sqlite3.exe"—that's your golden ticket. To make sure your computer knows where to find it, you might want to add it to your PATH (a list your system checks for programs). Here's how: right-click "This PC," choose "Properties," then "Advanced system settings," and click "Environment Variables." Find "Path" under "System variables," click "Edit," add "C:\SQLite," and hit OK all the way out. Now, open Command Prompt (type "cmd" in the Start menu), type "sqlite3 --version," and if you see "3.45" or similar, you're golden. If it says "not recognized," double-check that PATH addition or just run it directly from "C:\SQLite" with "cd C:\SQLite" then "sqlite3 --version."

Mac users, you've got it even easier. Open your Terminal (search "Terminal" in Spotlight), and type "sqlite3 --version." If you see a version number like "3.45," SQLite's already there—Apple often includes it. If you get "command not found," install it with Homebrew, a handy tool. First, set up Homebrew by pasting "/bin/bash -c "$(curl -fsSL https://raw.githubusercontent.com/Homebrew/install/HEAD/install.sh)"" into Terminal and following the prompts (it'll ask for your password). Once that's done, type "brew install sqlite" and wait a few minutes—then "sqlite3 --version" should work. Linux folks, open your terminal and try the same "sqlite3 --version" check. On Ubuntu, if it's missing, type "sudo apt update" then "sudo apt install sqlite3"—enter your password when asked. For Fedora, it's "sudo dnf install sqlite." Either way, you'll soon see that version number pop up.

Now, let's create a space to work. In your terminal (Command Prompt on Windows, Terminal on Mac/Linux), type "sqlite3 mydb.db"—this makes a new database file called "mydb.db" in whatever folder you're in. On Windows, you might start in "C:\Users\YourName"—use "cd C:\MySQLProjects" after making that folder to keep things tidy. You'll see a prompt: "sqlite>". That's where you'll type SQL commands. Try this: "CREATE TABLE test (id INTEGER, name TEXT);"—it builds a table called "test" with two columns. Then "INSERT INTO test VALUES (1, 'Liam');" adds a row. Type "SELECT * FROM test;" and you'll see "1 | Liam" (the "|" splits columns in the terminal). Type ".exit" to close it—your "mydb.db" file now holds that table. Reopen with "sqlite3 mydb.db" and "SELECT * FROM test;" again—it's still there!

For a prettier setup, download DB Browser for SQLite from sqlitebrowser.org. It's free and gives you a window to work in instead of a black terminal. Install it (double-click the downloaded file and follow the steps), then open it. Click "New Database," name it "mydb.db," and save it in "MySQLProjects." In the "Execute SQL" tab, type "CREATE TABLE test (id INTEGER, name TEXT);" and hit F5 or the play button—table created. Switch to "Browse Data"— nothing yet. Back to "Execute SQL," type "INSERT INTO test VALUES (1, 'Liam');" and run it. Now "Browse Data" shows "1" and "Liam" in a neat grid. Try "SELECT * FROM test;" in "Execute SQL"—same result below. If it's blank, check your semicolon—SQL needs it at the end of each command.

Let's test further: in terminal, "sqlite3 mydb.db," then "INSERT INTO test VALUES (2, 'Sarah');" and "SELECT * FROM test;"— you'll see two rows. In DB Browser, reopen "mydb.db" and run "SELECT * FROM test;"—same deal. If you get "database is locked," close DB Browser before using the terminal (only one can use it at a time). You've got SQL running, a database humming, and two ways to play with it—terminal for the purists, DB Browser for comfort. You're all set—fantastic work!

The Basics: Understanding Databases and Tables

Databases are the heart of SQL, and tables are how they organize data—think of them as tidy spreadsheets you can fill with whatever you like. Let's dig in and build some ourselves, so you can see how it all fits together. Open your terminal with "sqlite3 mydb.db" or fire up DB Browser and load "mydb.db." At the "sqlite>" prompt or in "Execute SQL," type: "CREATE TABLE friends (id INTEGER, name TEXT, age INTEGER);"—this creates a table called "friends" with three columns: "id" for numbers (like 1, 2, 3), "name" for text (like "Liam" or "Sarah"), and "age" for more numbers (like 25 or 30). Each column has a data type—INTEGER for whole numbers, TEXT for words or letters, and we'll see others soon. Hit enter (or F5 in DB Browser), and your table's ready—no error means success.

Now, let's add some data. Type "INSERT INTO friends VALUES (1, 'Sarah', 25);"—this slips one row into "friends": id 1, name Sarah, age 25. Check it with "SELECT * FROM friends;"—in the terminal, you'll see "1 | Sarah | 25" (those "|" marks split the columns), or in DB Browser, a nice row in "Browse Data." Add another: "INSERT INTO friends VALUES (2, 'Tom', 30);"—now "SELECT * FROM friends;" shows two rows: "1 | Sarah | 25" and "2 | Tom | 30." Each row is like a record card in that filing cabinet, and the columns are the labels on each field—id, name, age. You're telling SQL exactly what to store, and it keeps it neat.

Data types are key—they tell SQL what kind of info goes in each column. INTEGER is for numbers without decimals—perfect for ids or ages. TEXT handles anything you'd write, like names, addresses, or notes—no quotes needed when defining the column, but use them when adding data (e.g., 'Sarah'). There's also REAL for decimals—say you want to track heights: "CREATE TABLE heights (id INTEGER, name TEXT, height REAL);" then "INSERT INTO heights VALUES (1, 'Liam', 1.75);"—that's 1.75 meters. Check it: "SELECT * FROM heights;"—"1 | Liam | 1.75." Another type is BLOB for files (like photos), but we'll stick to basics for now.

Let's experiment. Back to "friends," try "INSERT INTO friends VALUES (3, 'Emma', 28);"—three friends now. What if you only want names? "SELECT name FROM friends;"—just "Sarah,"

"Tom," "Emma" (stacked in terminal, a column in DB Browser). Or names and ages: "SELECT name, age FROM friends;"—"Sarah | 25," "Tom | 30," "Emma | 28." You're picking what you see—SQL's flexible like that. Add a twist: "CREATE TABLE pets (id INTEGER, pet_name TEXT, owner_id INTEGER);" then "INSERT INTO pets VALUES (1, 'Fluffy', 2);"—Fluffy belongs to Tom (id 2). "SELECT * FROM pets;"—"1 | Fluffy | 2." Tables can relate—more on that later.

What happens if you mess up? Type "CREATE TABLE friends (id INTEGER);"—oops, "table friends already exists." Drop it first: "DROP TABLE friends;"—it's gone (check with "SELECT * FROM friends;"—"no such table"). Recreate: "CREATE TABLE friends (id INTEGER, name TEXT, age INTEGER);" and reload your data. Your work's saved in "mydb.db" as long as you don't delete that file—close with ".exit" and reopen anytime. Try "INSERT INTO friends VALUES (4, 'Aoife', 29);" then "SELECT * FROM friends WHERE age > 25;"—"Tom | 30," "Emma | 28," "Aoife | 29." If "no such table" pops up, you're in a new "mydb.db"—navigate to the right folder. You're building and filling tables—solid groundwork!

Simple Queries: Fetching Data with SELECT

SELECT is your go-to for pulling data out of tables—it's like asking your database, "What've you got for me?" Let's play with our "friends" table. Assuming it's got Sarah (1, 25), Tom (2, 30), Emma (3, 28), and Aoife (4, 29), type "SELECT * FROM friends;"—the "*" means "show me everything." Terminal gives "1 | Sarah | 25," "2 | Tom | 30," etc., while DB Browser lays it out in rows. That's your full roster—id, name, age, all at once.

But you don't always want everything. Try "SELECT name, age FROM friends;"—just names and ages: "Sarah | 25," "Tom | 30," "Emma | 28," "Aoife | 29." Skip id—maybe you're making a birthday list. Add more friends: "INSERT INTO friends VALUES (5, 'Mark', 27); INSERT INTO friends VALUES (6, 'Zoe', 31);." Now "SELECT name FROM friends WHERE age > 26;"—"Tom," "Emma," "Aoife," "Mark," "Zoe." The WHERE clause filters—only those over 26 show up. "SELECT id, name FROM friends WHERE name = 'Sarah';"— "1 | Sarah," pinpointing her. Use "!=" (not equal): "SELECT * FROM friends WHERE age != 25;"—everyone but Sarah.

Let's push it. "SELECT name, age FROM friends WHERE age < 30;"—Sarah (25), Emma (28), Mark (27), Aoife (29). What about exact matches? "SELECT * FROM friends WHERE id = 3;"—"3 | Emma | 28." Or ranges: "SELECT name FROM friends WHERE age >= 28 AND age <= 30;"—"Emma," "Tom," "Aoife." That "AND" combines rules—both must be true. Try "OR": "SELECT * FROM friends WHERE id = 1 OR id = 5;"—Sarah and Mark.

Mix it up: "CREATE TABLE books (id INTEGER, title TEXT, reader_id INTEGER); INSERT INTO books VALUES (1, 'Moby Dick', 2), (2, '1984', 4);." Then "SELECT title FROM books WHERE reader_id = 2;"—"Moby Dick" (Tom's reading). "SELECT * FROM books WHERE id > 1;"—"2 | 1984 | 4." In DB Browser, type these in "Execute SQL" and hit F5—results below. Terminal's the same—

just end with ";". If nothing shows, check your WHERE—maybe "age = 50" finds no one. Typo "SELECt" gives "syntax error"—fix it to "SELECT."

More examples: "SELECT name FROM friends WHERE name = 'Liam';"—empty unless I'm there (add me with "INSERT INTO friends VALUES (7, 'Liam', 32);"). "SELECT age FROM friends WHERE age < 0;"—nothing, no negative ages. "SELECT * FROM friends WHERE id <= 3;"—first three friends. You're asking precise questions—SQL's answering like a charm!

Filtering Data: Narrowing Down Your Results

Filtering with WHERE is how you zoom in on what matters—let's get good at it. With "friends" at Sarah (25), Tom (30), Emma (28), Aoife (29), Mark (27), Zoe (31), Liam (32), try "SELECT * FROM friends WHERE age < 30;"—Sarah, Emma, Mark, Aoife. Add complexity: "SELECT name FROM friends WHERE age > 25 AND age < 32;"—Tom, Emma, Aoife, Mark, Zoe. "AND" means both conditions must hold—over 25 but under 32. Now "OR": "SELECT * FROM friends WHERE id = 1 OR id = 5;"—Sarah and Mark, picking specific ids.

Wildcards with LIKE are handy. "SELECT name FROM friends WHERE name LIKE '%a';"—Sarah, Emma, Aoife—names ending in "a" ("%" means "anything before"). "SELECT name FROM friends WHERE name LIKE 'M%';"—Mark, starting with "M." "SELECT name FROM friends WHERE name LIKE '%ar%';"—Sarah, Mark—containing "ar" anywhere. Case matters in some systems, but SQLite's lenient—'m%' or 'M%' both catch Mark.

Ranges with BETWEEN: "SELECT * FROM friends WHERE age BETWEEN 25 AND 30;"—Sarah (25), Tom (30), Emma (28), Mark (27), Aoife (29)—inclusive at both ends. "SELECT name FROM friends WHERE id BETWEEN 2 AND 4;"—Tom, Emma, Aoife. Combine: "SELECT * FROM friends WHERE age BETWEEN 26 AND 29 AND name LIKE '%e';"—Mark (27), Aoife (29)—age fit plus "e" ending.

Negatives: "SELECT name FROM friends WHERE age NOT BETWEEN 25 AND 30;"—Zoe (31), Liam (32). "SELECT * FROM friends WHERE name NOT LIKE '%a';"—Tom, Mark, Zoe, Liam—no "a" at the end. Add data: "INSERT INTO friends VALUES (8, 'Kate', 26);"—then "SELECT * FROM friends WHERE age < 28 OR name = 'Tom';"—Sarah, Tom, Mark, Kate. If it's blank, check conditions— "age > 50" finds nothing here. "SELECT name FROM friends WHERE id IN (1, 3, 5);"—Sarah, Emma, Mark—specific ids. You're slicing data like a pro—keep practicing!

Adding Data: Inserting Information into Tables

Alright, let's get to the fun part—adding data to your tables with the INSERT command! This is where your database starts to come alive, growing from an empty shell into something useful and full of information. Whether you're tracking friends, planning a trip, or cataloging your favorite books, INSERT is how you fill those tables up, row by row. I'll walk you through it slowly and clearly, with plenty of examples to try, so you can see how flexible and powerful this command can be. By the end, you'll be popping data into your database like a pro, and I'll be right here cheering you on—let's dive in!

Assuming you've got your "friends" table from earlier—set up with "CREATE TABLE friends (id INTEGER, name TEXT, age INTEGER);"—let's start simple. The most straightforward way to add data is to list all the columns and their values in order. Type this at your "sqlite>" prompt in the terminal or in DB Browser's "Execute SQL" tab: "INSERT INTO friends (id, name, age) VALUES (1, 'Sarah', 25);". Hit enter (or F5 in DB Browser), and that's it—one row added! To check, run "SELECT * FROM friends;"—you'll see "1 | Sarah | 25" in the terminal (those "|" marks separate columns) or a neat row in DB Browser's "Browse Data" tab. What's happening here? You're telling SQL: "Put this data into the 'friends' table—id is 1, name is Sarah, age is 25." The columns (id, name, age) match the VALUES (1, 'Sarah', 25) one-to-one, and SQLite tucks it away in "mydb.db" for you.

Let's add more. Try "INSERT INTO friends (id, name, age) VALUES (2, 'Tom', 30);"—another friend joins the crew. Check again with "SELECT * FROM friends;"—now it's "1 | Sarah | 25" and "2 | Tom | 30." Notice the pattern: you name the table (friends), list the columns in parentheses, then provide the values in the same order, wrapped in VALUES. The quotes around text like 'Sarah' or 'Tom' are crucial—TEXT data needs them, while numbers like 1 or 30 don't. What if you forget quotes? Try "INSERT INTO friends (id, name, age) VALUES (3, Emma, 28);"—you'll get a "syntax error near 'Emma'" because SQLite thinks Emma's a command, not a name. Fix it: "INSERT INTO friends (id, name, age) VALUES (3, 'Emma', 28);"—now "SELECT * FROM friends;" shows three rows.

You don't always have to list every column, though—that's where INSERT gets flexible. Say you don't know the id yet, or you want it to fill in later (we'll tweak that soon). Type "INSERT INTO friends (name, age) VALUES ('Aoife', 29);"—just name and age. Check it: "SELECT * FROM friends;"—you'll see something like "1 | Sarah | 25," "2 | Tom | 30," "3 | Emma | 28," and " | Aoife | 29" (that blank spot is a NULL id—SQLite leaves it empty if unspecified). This is handy if some data's optional or missing. Add another: "INSERT INTO friends (name, age) VALUES ('Mark', 27);"—five friends now. Order doesn't matter either: "INSERT INTO friends (age, name) VALUES (31, 'Zoe');"—still works, as long as the values match the columns you named. "SELECT * FROM friends WHERE name = 'Zoe';"—" | Zoe | 31."

What about adding multiple rows at once? SQLite lets you stack them in one go—super time-saver! Try "INSERT INTO friends (name, age) VALUES ('John', 33), ('Ellen', 24), ('Pat', 35);"—three rows in one command. Run "SELECT * FROM friends;"—you'll see all eight now (if you've followed along): Sarah, Tom, Emma, Aoife, Mark, Zoe, John, Ellen, Pat. In DB Browser, this works smoothly—type it, hit F5, and watch "Browse Data" fill up. In the terminal, some older SQLite versions might hiccup, so you'd split it: "INSERT INTO friends (name, age) VALUES ('John', 33);" then "INSERT INTO friends (name, age) VALUES ('Ellen', 24);" and so on. Either way, your table's growing fast!

Let's mix it up with a new table—say you're planning trips. Type "CREATE TABLE trips (id INTEGER, destination TEXT, friend_id INTEGER);"—id for the trip, destination as text, friend_id linking to "friends." Add some: "INSERT INTO trips (id, destination, friend_id) VALUES (1, 'Paris', 1);"—Sarah's off to Paris. "SELECT * FROM trips;"—"1 | Paris | 1." Keep going: "INSERT INTO trips (id, destination, friend_id) VALUES (2, 'London', 3), (3, 'Rome', 5);"— Emma's to London, Mark's to Rome. "SELECT * FROM trips;"— three trips listed. Partial again: "INSERT INTO trips (destination, friend_id) VALUES ('Berlin', 2);"—Tom's trip, id NULL for now.

Errors can pop up—let's handle them. Try "INSERT INTO trips VALUES (4, 'Dublin');"—"column count doesn't match value count." You gave two values (4, 'Dublin') but trips has three columns (id, destination, friend_id). Fix it: "INSERT INTO trips VALUES (4, 'Dublin', 4);"—Aoife's trip. Or specify: "INSERT INTO trips (id, destination, friend_id) VALUES (4, 'Dublin', 4);"—same result. What if you typo a column? "INSERT INTO trips (id, dest, friend_id) VALUES (5, 'Madrid', 5);"—"no such column: dest." Correct it: "destination," not "dest."

Let's add variety. "CREATE TABLE books (id INTEGER, title TEXT, pages INTEGER, reader_id INTEGER);"—for your reading list. "INSERT INTO books (id, title, pages, reader_id) VALUES (1, 'Moby Dick', 635, 2);"—Tom's book. "INSERT INTO books (title, pages, reader_id) VALUES ('1984', 328, 4);"—Aoife's, id NULL. Multiple: "INSERT INTO books (title, pages, reader_id) VALUES ('The Hobbit', 310, 1), ('Dune', 412, 3);"—Sarah and Emma join in. "SELECT * FROM books;"—four books, some with ids, some without.

Now, let's make ids smarter with PRIMARY KEY—it auto-increments, saving you from typing them. Drop "friends" first: "DROP TABLE friends;"—then recreate: "CREATE TABLE friends (id INTEGER PRIMARY KEY, name TEXT, age INTEGER);." Now

"INSERT INTO friends (name, age) VALUES ('Liam', 32);"—no id needed. "SELECT * FROM friends;"—"1 | Liam | 32," id starts at 1. Add more: "INSERT INTO friends (name, age) VALUES ('Kate', 26), ('Sean', 29);"—"2 | Kate | 26," "3 | Sean | 29." Even with PRIMARY KEY, you can set id: "INSERT INTO friends (id, name, age) VALUES (10, 'Clare', 23);"—"10 | Clare | 23," then "INSERT INTO friends (name, age) VALUES ('Pat', 35);"—id jumps to 11.

Real-world scenario: a shop inventory. "CREATE TABLE inventory (item_id INTEGER PRIMARY KEY, item_name TEXT, quantity INTEGER);." Stock it: "INSERT INTO inventory (item_name, quantity) VALUES ('Bread', 50), ('Milk', 30), ('Eggs', 100);"—"1 | Bread | 50," etc. "INSERT INTO inventory (item_id, item_name, quantity) VALUES (10, 'Cheese', 20);"—specific id. "SELECT * FROM inventory;"—your shop's stocked!

One more: a diary. "CREATE TABLE diary (entry_id INTEGER PRIMARY KEY, date TEXT, note TEXT);." "INSERT INTO diary (date, note) VALUES ('2025-04-06', 'Sunny day in Galway'), ('2025-04-07', 'Coded all morning');"—"1 | 2025-04-06 | Sunny day in Galway," etc. "INSERT INTO diary (entry_id, date, note) VALUES (5, '2025-04-08', 'Tea with Aoife');"—custom id. Your diary's filling up!

If "UNIQUE constraint failed" appears with PRIMARY KEY, you tried reusing an id—skip it or let it auto-increment. "SELECT * FROM" confirms every addition—your data's safe in "mydb.db." You're building a bustling database—fantastic work!

Changing Data: Updating and Deleting Records

Now that you've got data in your tables, let's talk about how to change it—because life's rarely set in stone, and neither is your database! Whether you've made a typo, need to update someone's age, or want to clear out old records, SQL's got two trusty tools for the job: UPDATE for tweaking what's there, and DELETE for removing what's not needed anymore. This is where you take control, shaping your data to match reality, and I'll guide you through it with plenty of examples to try. We'll go slow, build your confidence, and make sure you're comfortable fixing things up— let's get started, shall we?

Let's assume you've got your "friends" table humming along from the last section, set up with "CREATE TABLE friends (id INTEGER PRIMARY KEY, name TEXT, age INTEGER);" and filled with a few rows—say, "1 | Liam | 32," "2 | Kate | 26," "3 | Sean | 29," "10 | Clare | 23," "11 | Pat | 35" (added via INSERT with PRIMARY KEY auto-incrementing where needed). You can check it with "SELECT * FROM friends;" in your terminal (at "sqlite>") or DB Browser's "Browse Data" tab. If it's not there, recreate it with that CREATE command and pop in some data—your playground's ready!

Updating with UPDATE

First up, UPDATE—perfect for fixing mistakes or reflecting changes. Say Kate just had a birthday—time to bump her age. Type "UPDATE friends SET age = 27 WHERE name = 'Kate';" and hit enter (or F5 in DB Browser). What's this doing? UPDATE targets the "friends" table, SET tells SQL what to change (age to 27), and WHERE pinpoints which row (Kate's, by name). Run "SELECT * FROM friends WHERE name = 'Kate';"—now it's "2 | Kate | 27." Brilliant—she's updated! Without WHERE, it'd change every row— dangerous stuff—so always double-check that part.

Let's tweak more. Maybe you misspelled Clare as "Claire" earlier. Fix it: "UPDATE friends SET name = 'Clare' WHERE id = 10;"—id's unique, so it's a safe bet. "SELECT * FROM friends WHERE id = 10;"—"10 | Clare | 23," spot on. What if everyone under 30 gets a year older? "UPDATE friends SET age = age + 1 WHERE age < 30;"—Kate's now 28, Sean's 30, Clare's 24. Check it: "SELECT * FROM friends WHERE age < 31;"—see the updates. That "age = age + 1" is neat—it takes the current value and adds 1, like a little math trick inside SQL.

You can change multiple columns too. Suppose Pat's moving up in the world—new name, new age: "UPDATE friends SET name = 'Patrick', age = 36 WHERE id = 11;"—"SELECT * FROM friends WHERE id = 11;"—"11 | Patrick | 36." Or tweak based on patterns: "UPDATE friends SET age = 25 WHERE name LIKE '%e';"—Kate (ending in "e") and Clare (has an "e") both become 25. "SELECT * FROM friends WHERE name LIKE '%e';"—confirm it. Be careful—LIKE catches more than you might expect!

What if nothing changes? "UPDATE friends SET age = 40 WHERE name = 'Aoife';"—"SELECT * FROM friends WHERE name = 'Aoife';"—empty? Aoife's not there—check your data with "SELECT * FROM friends;." Or "UPDATE friends SET age = 30 WHERE age > 50;"—no one's over 50, so no effect. WHERE's your filter—get it wrong, and SQL shrugs.

Real-World Updates

Let's try a shop scenario. "CREATE TABLE inventory (item_id INTEGER PRIMARY KEY, item_name TEXT, quantity INTEGER);" then "INSERT INTO inventory (item_name, quantity) VALUES ('Bread', 50), ('Milk', 30), ('Eggs', 100);." Sold some bread? "UPDATE inventory SET quantity = 45 WHERE item_name = 'Bread';"—"SELECT * FROM inventory WHERE item_name = 'Bread';"—"1 | Bread | 45." Restock milk: "UPDATE inventory SET quantity = quantity + 20 WHERE item_name = 'Milk';"—now 50. "SELECT * FROM inventory;"—all updated. Typo fix: "UPDATE inventory SET item_name = 'Eggs' WHERE item_name = 'Egs';"— no change unless "Egs" exists—check first!

Another case: a diary. "CREATE TABLE diary (entry_id INTEGER PRIMARY KEY, date TEXT, note TEXT); INSERT INTO diary (date, note) VALUES ('2025-04-06', 'Sunny day'), ('2025-04-07', 'Coded');." Edit: "UPDATE diary SET note = 'Sunny day in Galway' WHERE date = '2025-04-06';"—"SELECT * FROM diary WHERE date = '2025-04-06';"—"1 | 2025-04-06 | Sunny day in Galway." Add detail: "UPDATE diary SET note = note || ' all morning' WHERE entry_id = 2;"—that "||" joins text, so "2 | 2025-04-07 | Coded all morning."

Deleting with DELETE

Now, DELETE—when you need to clear out data. Maybe Sean's left the group: "DELETE FROM friends WHERE id = 3;"—"SELECT * FROM friends WHERE id = 3;"—gone! "SELECT * FROM friends;"—just Liam, Kate, Clare, Patrick now (assuming earlier updates). Delete by age: "DELETE FROM friends WHERE age > 30;"—Liam (32) and Patrick (36) vanish. "SELECT * FROM friends;"—Kate (25), Clare (25) remain. No WHERE? "DELETE FROM friends;"—wipes the whole table—use cautiously (redo inserts if you try it)!

Back to inventory: sold out of eggs? "DELETE FROM inventory WHERE item_name = 'Eggs';"—"SELECT * FROM inventory;"— Bread and Milk only. Low stock? "DELETE FROM inventory WHERE quantity < 10;"—nothing yet, but if Milk drops to 5 later, it's out. Diary cleanup: "DELETE FROM diary WHERE date = '2025-04-06';"—that sunny day's erased. "SELECT * FROM diary;"—just the coding entry.

Combining and Testing

Mix it: "UPDATE inventory SET quantity = 0 WHERE item_name = 'Milk';" then "DELETE FROM inventory WHERE quantity = 0;"— Milk's gone after setting it to zero. "SELECT * FROM inventory;"— Bread alone. Friends example: "UPDATE friends SET age = 50 WHERE name = 'Kate';" then "DELETE FROM friends WHERE age > 40;"—Kate's out. Recreate her: "INSERT INTO friends (name, age) VALUES ('Kate', 26);."

Errors? "DELETE FROM friends WHERE name = 'Bob';"—no Bob, no change. "UPDATE friends SET ages = 30 WHERE id = 1;"—"no such column: ages"—typo, fix to "age." "DELETE FROM friend;"— "no such table"—it's "friends." Check "SELECT * FROM" after each change—empty means success (for DELETE) or a miss.

Advanced Tweaks

Add a column: "ALTER TABLE friends ADD COLUMN city TEXT;"—then "UPDATE friends SET city = 'Galway' WHERE id = 1;"—Liam's in Galway. "UPDATE friends SET city = 'Dublin' WHERE age < 30;"—Kate and Clare move. "SELECT * FROM friends;"—new column filled. Clear cities: "UPDATE friends SET city = NULL WHERE city = 'Dublin';"—back to blank. "DELETE FROM friends WHERE city IS NULL;"—Kate and Clare gone again.

Try trips: "CREATE TABLE trips (id INTEGER PRIMARY KEY, destination TEXT, friend_id INTEGER); INSERT INTO trips VALUES (1, 'Paris', 1), (2, 'London', 2);." Cancel Paris: "DELETE FROM trips WHERE destination = 'Paris';"—"SELECT * FROM trips;"—London's left. Update: "UPDATE trips SET destination = 'Rome' WHERE friend_id = 2;"—Kate's rerouted.

Practical Scenarios

Book club: "CREATE TABLE books (id INTEGER PRIMARY KEY, title TEXT, reader_id INTEGER); INSERT INTO books VALUES (1, 'Dune', 1), (2, '1984', 2);." Finish a book: "ALTER TABLE books

ADD COLUMN finished INTEGER DEFAULT 0;"—"UPDATE books SET finished = 1 WHERE title = 'Dune';"—"SELECT * FROM books;"—"1 | Dune | 1 | 1." Drop finished: "DELETE FROM books WHERE finished = 1;"—Dune's out.

Budget tracker: "CREATE TABLE expenses (id INTEGER PRIMARY KEY, item TEXT, cost REAL); INSERT INTO expenses VALUES (1, 'Rent', 500.50), (2, 'Food', 75.25);." Adjust: "UPDATE expenses SET cost = 550.00 WHERE item = 'Rent';"—"SELECT * FROM expenses;"—updated. Cut small costs: "DELETE FROM expenses WHERE cost < 100;"—Food's gone.

Your data's fluid now—UPDATE and DELETE let you adapt it to anything. "SELECT * FROM" is your mirror—reflects every change. You're reshaping your database like a master—well done!

Joining Tables: Connecting Information Like a Pro

Welcome to one of the most exciting parts of SQL—joining tables! This is where your database starts to feel like a living, breathing thing, with bits of information linking up to tell a bigger story. If you've ever wondered how to connect who's going on a trip with where they're headed, or which friend borrowed which book, JOIN is your answer. It's like being a detective, piecing together clues from different files, and I'm here to guide you through it step by step. We'll explore different types of joins, try them out with plenty of examples, and make sure you're comfortable linking data like a pro. Don't worry if it sounds tricky—I'll keep it clear and fun, and by the end, you'll be amazed at what you can do. Ready to connect the dots? Let's dive in!

Let's start with our "friends" table from earlier, assuming it's set up as "CREATE TABLE friends (id INTEGER PRIMARY KEY, name TEXT, age INTEGER);" with some data: "1 | Liam | 32," "2 | Kate | 26," "3 | Sean | 29," "4 | Clare | 23." Check it with "SELECT * FROM friends;" in your terminal (at "sqlite>") or DB Browser's "Browse Data" tab. If it's not there, recreate it and pop in those rows with INSERT—your base is ready. Now, let's pair it with something else—say, hobbies. Type "CREATE TABLE hobbies (friend_id INTEGER, hobby TEXT);" then add some rows: "INSERT INTO hobbies VALUES (1, 'reading'), (2, 'gaming'), (3, 'coding');." "SELECT * FROM hobbies;"—"1 | reading," "2 | gaming," "3 | coding." Here, friend_id links to the id in "friends"—Liam reads, Kate games, Sean codes, but Clare's hobby-free for now.

The Basic JOIN (INNER JOIN)

The simplest join is an INNER JOIN—it finds matches between tables. Try this: "SELECT friends.name, hobbies.hobby FROM friends JOIN hobbies ON friends.id = hobbies.friend_id;"—run it, and you'll see "Liam | reading," "Kate | gaming," "Sean | coding."

What's happening? FROM friends JOIN hobbies says "pair these tables," and ON friends.id = hobbies.friend_id tells SQL how— match each friend's id with the hobby's friend_id. The SELECT picks what to show: names from "friends," hobbies from "hobbies." Clare's missing—INNER JOIN only includes rows with matches in both tables. In DB Browser, type this in "Execute SQL" and hit F5— same result in a neat grid. Terminal shows "|" between columns— your data's linked!

Let's tweak it. "SELECT friends.name, friends.age, hobbies.hobby FROM friends JOIN hobbies ON friends.id = hobbies.friend_id;"— now "Liam | 32 | reading," "Kate | 26 | gaming," "Sean | 29 | coding." Add more hobbies: "INSERT INTO hobbies VALUES (1, 'hiking');"—Liam's got two. Run the join again— "Liam | 32 | reading," "Liam | 32 | hiking," "Kate | 26 | gaming," "Sean | 29 | coding." One-to-many works—each friend can have multiple hobbies.

LEFT JOIN: Keeping Everyone

What about Clare? INNER JOIN skips her—no hobby match. Try a LEFT JOIN: "SELECT friends.name, hobbies.hobby FROM friends LEFT JOIN hobbies ON friends.id = hobbies.friend_id;"—"Liam | reading," "Liam | hiking," "Kate | gaming," "Sean | coding," "Clare | NULL." LEFT JOIN keeps all rows from the left table ("friends"), adding NULL where there's no match in "hobbies." Clare's here, hobby-less. Add "SELECT friends.id, friends.name, hobbies.hobby FROM friends LEFT JOIN hobbies ON friends.id = hobbies.friend_id;"—ids show too: "1 | Liam | reading," "1 | Liam | hiking," "2 | Kate | gaming," "3 | Sean | coding," "4 | Clare | NULL."

Filter it: "SELECT friends.name, hobbies.hobby FROM friends LEFT JOIN hobbies ON friends.id = hobbies.friend_id WHERE hobbies.hobby IS NULL;"—"Clare | NULL." This finds friends without hobbies—handy! Add "INSERT INTO hobbies VALUES (4, 'painting');"—rerun the full LEFT JOIN: Clare's got "4 | Clare | painting" now, no NULL.

RIGHT JOIN and More Hobbies

SQLite doesn't support RIGHT JOIN natively, but we can flip it: "SELECT friends.name, hobbies.hobby FROM hobbies LEFT JOIN friends ON hobbies.friend_id = friends.id;"—same effect. It keeps all hobbies, NULL for unmatched friends. Add an orphan hobby: "INSERT INTO hobbies VALUES (5, 'swimming');"—no friend 5 exists. Run it— "Liam | reading," "Liam | hiking," "Kate | gaming," "Sean | coding," "Clare | painting," "NULL | swimming." Useful for spotting unpaired data!

Multiple Tables: Trips Too

Let's add trips: "CREATE TABLE trips (id INTEGER PRIMARY KEY, destination TEXT, friend_id INTEGER); INSERT INTO trips VALUES (1, 'Paris', 1), (2, 'London', 2), (3, 'Rome', 4);." Join friends and trips: "SELECT friends.name, trips.destination FROM friends JOIN trips ON friends.id = trips.friend_id;"—"Liam | Paris," "Kate | London," "Clare | Rome." Sean's trip-less—INNER JOIN skips him. LEFT JOIN: "SELECT friends.name, trips.destination FROM friends LEFT JOIN trips ON friends.id = trips.friend_id;"—Sean's "Sean | NULL" joins the list.

Now, three tables! "SELECT friends.name, hobbies.hobby, trips.destination FROM friends LEFT JOIN hobbies ON friends.id = hobbies.friend_id LEFT JOIN trips ON friends.id = trips.friend_id;"— "Liam | reading | Paris," "Liam | hiking | Paris," "Kate | gaming | London," "Sean | coding | NULL," "Clare | painting | Rome." Multiple LEFT JOINs stack—Liam's Paris repeats per hobby, Sean's trip-less, all connected.

Practical Scenarios

Book club: "CREATE TABLE books (id INTEGER PRIMARY KEY, title TEXT, reader_id INTEGER); INSERT INTO books VALUES (1, 'Dune', 1), (2, '1984', 2);." Join: "SELECT friends.name, books.title FROM friends JOIN books ON friends.id = books.reader_id;"—"Liam | Dune," "Kate | 1984." LEFT JOIN: "SELECT friends.name, books.title FROM friends LEFT JOIN books ON friends.id = books.reader_id;"—Sean and Clare get NULL titles.

Inventory sales: "CREATE TABLE sales (sale_id INTEGER PRIMARY KEY, item_id INTEGER, quantity INTEGER); INSERT INTO sales VALUES (1, 1, 5), (2, 2, 10); CREATE TABLE inventory (item_id INTEGER PRIMARY KEY, item_name TEXT); INSERT INTO inventory VALUES (1, 'Bread'), (2, 'Milk'), (3, 'Eggs');." Join: "SELECT inventory.item_name, sales.quantity FROM inventory JOIN sales ON inventory.item_id = sales.item_id;"—"Bread | 5," "Milk | 10." LEFT JOIN: "SELECT inventory.item_name, sales.quantity FROM inventory LEFT JOIN sales ON inventory.item_id = sales.item_id;"—"Eggs | NULL" joins in.

Event RSVPs: "CREATE TABLE events (event_id INTEGER PRIMARY KEY, event_name TEXT); INSERT INTO events VALUES (1, 'Party'), (2, 'Hike'); CREATE TABLE rsvps (friend_id INTEGER, event_id INTEGER); INSERT INTO rsvps VALUES (1, 1), (2, 1), (3, 2);." Join: "SELECT friends.name, events.event_name FROM friends JOIN rsvps ON friends.id = rsvps.friend_id JOIN events ON rsvps.event_id = events.event_id;"—"Liam | Party," "Kate | Party," "Sean | Hike." LEFT JOIN from friends: "SELECT friends.name, events.event_name FROM friends LEFT JOIN rsvps ON friends.id = rsvps.friend_id LEFT JOIN events ON rsvps.event_id = events.event_id;"—Clare's "Clare | NULL."

Troubleshooting Joins

Empty result? "SELECT friends.name, hobbies.hobby FROM friends JOIN hobbies ON friends.id = hobbies.friend_id;"—if blank, check friend_id values—typos like "INSERT INTO hobbies VALUES (10, 'singing');" (no friend 10) fail INNER JOIN. "SELECT * FROM hobbies;"—confirm matches. Too many rows? Multiple hobbies per friend—normal with one-to-many. "SELECT DISTINCT friends.name, trips.destination FROM friends JOIN trips ON friends.id = trips.friend_id;"—cuts duplicates if needed.

Add conditions: "SELECT friends.name, hobbies.hobby FROM friends JOIN hobbies ON friends.id = hobbies.friend_id WHERE friends.age > 28;"—"Liam | reading," "Liam | hiking," "Sean | coding." Join with aggregates: "SELECT friends.name, COUNT(hobbies.hobby) AS hobby_count FROM friends LEFT JOIN hobbies ON friends.id = hobbies.friend_id GROUP BY friends.id, friends.name;"—counts hobbies per friend.

Advanced Joins

Self-join for mentors: "ALTER TABLE friends ADD COLUMN mentor_id INTEGER; UPDATE friends SET mentor_id = 1 WHERE id = 2; UPDATE friends SET mentor_id = 3 WHERE id = 4;." "SELECT f1.name AS friend, f2.name AS mentor FROM friends f1 LEFT JOIN friends f2 ON f1.mentor_id = f2.id;"—"Liam | NULL," "Kate | Liam," "Sean | NULL," "Clare | Sean." Aliases (f1, f2) keep it clear.

Your tables are talking now—INNER JOIN for matches, LEFT JOIN for all, multi-table for big pictures. "SELECT * FROM" each table, then join—see the magic! You're a data connector extraordinaire— well done!

Aggregates: Summing, Counting, and Averaging

Welcome to the world of aggregates—where SQL turns your data into answers! If you've ever wanted to know how many friends you've got, what their average age is, or the total cost of your shopping, aggregate functions are your go-to tools. They crunch numbers and summarize information, saving you from tedious manual tallies. I'm excited to walk you through this—it's like giving your database a calculator and a notepad, and I'll make sure it's clear and fun. We'll explore COUNT, SUM, AVG, and more, with heaps of examples to try, so you can see how they work in real life. Let's roll up our sleeves and start summing things up—ready?

Let's assume your "friends" table is set up from earlier: "CREATE TABLE friends (id INTEGER PRIMARY KEY, name TEXT, age INTEGER);" with data like "1 | Liam | 32," "2 | Kate | 26," "3 | Sean | 29," "4 | Clare | 23," "5 | Pat | 35." Check it with "SELECT * FROM friends;" in your terminal (at "sqlite>") or DB Browser's "Browse Data" tab. If it's not there, recreate it and INSERT those rows—your sandbox is primed!

Counting with COUNT

First up, COUNT—perfect for tallying rows. Type "SELECT COUNT() FROM friends;"—you'll get "5" (or however many rows you've got). That "" means "count every row, no matter what's in it." Simple, right? Run it in DB Browser's "Execute SQL" (hit F5) or terminal—same result, a single number. What if you only want friends over 25? "SELECT COUNT(*) FROM friends WHERE age > 25;"—"4" (Liam 32, Kate 26, Sean 29, Pat 35—Clare's 23 misses out). WHERE filters before counting—handy!

You can count specific columns too. "SELECT COUNT(age) FROM friends;"—still "5," since all have ages. Add a twist: "ALTER TABLE friends ADD COLUMN city TEXT; UPDATE friends SET city = 'Galway' WHERE id IN (1, 3);"—now Liam and Sean have cities.

"SELECT COUNT(city) FROM friends;"—"2," because COUNT skips NULLs (Kate, Clare, Pat lack cities). Compare: "SELECT COUNT() FROM friends WHERE city IS NOT NULL;"—also "2." Label it: "SELECT COUNT() AS total_friends FROM friends;"— "total_friends | 5"—nicer to read!

Summing with SUM

Next, SUM—adds up numbers. "SELECT SUM(age) FROM friends;"—32 + 26 + 29 + 23 + 35 = 145. "SELECT SUM(age) AS total_age FROM friends;"—"total_age | 145." Filter it: "SELECT SUM(age) FROM friends WHERE age < 30;"—Kate (26), Sean (29), Clare (23) = 78. "SELECT SUM(age) AS young_total FROM friends WHERE age < 30;"—"young_total | 78." What if no rows match? "SELECT SUM(age) FROM friends WHERE age > 50;"— "NULL"—no data, no sum.

Try a budget: "CREATE TABLE expenses (id INTEGER PRIMARY KEY, item TEXT, cost REAL); INSERT INTO expenses VALUES (1, 'Rent', 500.50), (2, 'Food', 75.25), (3, 'Bus', 20.00);." "SELECT SUM(cost) FROM expenses;"—595.75. "SELECT SUM(cost) AS weekly_total FROM expenses WHERE item != 'Rent';"—Food + Bus = 95.25. Real numbers (REAL type) work fine—decimals included!

Averaging with AVG

AVG gives you the mean. "SELECT AVG(age) FROM friends;"— 145 ÷ 5 = 29.0. "SELECT AVG(age) AS avg_age FROM friends;"— "avg_age | 29.0." Filter: "SELECT AVG(age) FROM friends WHERE age > 25;"—(32 + 26 + 29 + 35) ÷ 4 = 30.5. Round it: "SELECT ROUND(AVG(age), 1) AS avg_age FROM friends WHERE age > 25;"—"avg_age | 30.5" (ROUND keeps one decimal). "SELECT AVG(age) FROM friends WHERE age < 20;"— "NULL"—no matches.

Back to expenses: "SELECT AVG(cost) FROM expenses;"—595.75 ÷ 3 ≈ 198.5833. "SELECT ROUND(AVG(cost), 2) AS avg_cost FROM expenses;"—"avg_cost | 198.58." Filter: "SELECT AVG(cost) FROM expenses WHERE cost < 100;"—(75.25 + 20.00) ÷ 2 = 47.625, rounded to "47.63." AVG's your quick stats tool!

Max and Min with MAX and MIN

MAX finds the biggest, MIN the smallest. "SELECT MAX(age) FROM friends;"—35 (Pat). "SELECT MIN(age) FROM friends;"—23 (Clare). Label: "SELECT MAX(age) AS oldest, MIN(age) AS youngest FROM friends;"—"oldest | 35 | youngest | 23" in one go! Filter: "SELECT MAX(cost) FROM expenses WHERE cost < 500;"—75.25. "SELECT MIN(cost) FROM expenses;"—20.00.

Grouping with Aggregates

Aggregates shine with GROUP BY—summarize by category. Add cities: "UPDATE friends SET city = 'Dublin' WHERE id IN (2, 4); UPDATE friends SET city = 'Cork' WHERE id = 5;." "SELECT city, COUNT(*) AS friend_count FROM friends GROUP BY city;"—"Galway | 2," "Dublin | 2," "Cork | 1." "SELECT city, AVG(age) AS avg_age FROM friends GROUP BY city;"—"Galway | 30.5," "Dublin | 24.5," "Cork | 35.0." Add WHERE: "SELECT city, SUM(age) AS total_age FROM friends WHERE age > 25 GROUP BY city;"—"Galway | 61," "Dublin | 26," "Cork | 35."

Expenses by type: "ALTER TABLE expenses ADD COLUMN category TEXT; UPDATE expenses SET category = 'Home' WHERE id = 1; UPDATE expenses SET category = 'Daily' WHERE id IN (2, 3);." "SELECT category, SUM(cost) AS total FROM expenses GROUP BY category;"—"Home | 500.50," "Daily | 95.25." "SELECT category, COUNT(*) AS items FROM expenses GROUP BY category;"—"Home | 1," "Daily | 2."

Joining with Aggregates

Pair with "trips": "CREATE TABLE trips (id INTEGER PRIMARY KEY, destination TEXT, friend_id INTEGER); INSERT INTO trips VALUES (1, 'Paris', 1), (2, 'London', 2), (3, 'Rome', 4);." "SELECT friends.name, COUNT(trips.id) AS trip_count FROM friends LEFT JOIN trips ON friends.id = trips.friend_id GROUP BY friends.id, friends.name;"—"Liam | 1," "Kate | 1," "Sean | 0," "Clare | 1," "Pat | 0." LEFT JOIN ensures all friends, even trip-less ones.

Books: "CREATE TABLE books (id INTEGER PRIMARY KEY, title TEXT, reader_id INTEGER, pages INTEGER); INSERT INTO books VALUES (1, 'Dune', 1, 412), (2, '1984', 2, 328), (3, 'Hobbit', 1, 310);." "SELECT friends.name, SUM(books.pages) AS total_pages FROM friends LEFT JOIN books ON friends.id = books.reader_id GROUP BY friends.name;"—"Liam | 722," "Kate | 328," "Sean | NULL," "Clare | NULL," "Pat | NULL." "SELECT friends.name, AVG(books.pages) AS avg_pages FROM friends LEFT JOIN books ON friends.id = books.reader_id GROUP BY friends.name;"—"Liam | 361.0," "Kate | 328.0," etc.

Practical Scenarios

Shop sales: "CREATE TABLE sales (sale_id INTEGER PRIMARY KEY, item_id INTEGER, quantity INTEGER); INSERT INTO sales VALUES (1, 1, 5), (2, 1, 10), (3, 2, 8); CREATE TABLE items (item_id INTEGER PRIMARY KEY, item_name TEXT); INSERT INTO items VALUES (1, 'Bread'), (2, 'Milk');." "SELECT items.item_name, SUM(sales.quantity) AS total_sold FROM items LEFT JOIN sales ON items.item_id = sales.item_id GROUP BY items.item_name;"—"Bread | 15," "Milk | 8." "SELECT COUNT(sale_id) AS sales_count FROM sales;"—"3."

Event RSVPs: "CREATE TABLE events (event_id INTEGER PRIMARY KEY, event_name TEXT); INSERT INTO events VALUES (1, 'Party'), (2, 'Hike'); CREATE TABLE rsvps (friend_id INTEGER, event_id INTEGER); INSERT INTO rsvps VALUES (1,

1), (2, 1), (3, 2), (4, 1);." "SELECT events.event_name, COUNT(rsvps.friend_id) AS attendees FROM events LEFT JOIN rsvps ON events.event_id = rsvps.event_id GROUP BY events.event_name;"—"Party | 3," "Hike | 1."

Daily log: "CREATE TABLE log (log_id INTEGER PRIMARY KEY, date TEXT, hours REAL); INSERT INTO log VALUES (1, '2025-04-06', 2.5), (2, '2025-04-06', 1.5), (3, '2025-04-07', 3.0);." "SELECT date, SUM(hours) AS total_hours FROM log GROUP BY date;"—"2025-04-06 | 4.0," "2025-04-07 | 3.0." "SELECT AVG(hours) AS avg_hours FROM log;"—"2.3333" (round it if you like).

Troubleshooting

"NULL" result? "SELECT SUM(age) FROM friends WHERE age > 50;"—no matches. Wrong count? "SELECT COUNT(city) FROM friends;"—skips NULLs, use "" for all rows. GROUP BY oddities? "SELECT name, COUNT() FROM friends;"—error, name needs GROUP BY too. Check data with "SELECT * FROM"—ensures your base count on aggregates to shine! You're summarizing like a champ—fantastic work!

Organizing Data: Sorting and Grouping Results

Alright, let's bring some order to your data! Once you've got tables full of information, you'll want to sort it into a neat lineup or group it into meaningful chunks—SQL's got just the tools for that with ORDER BY and GROUP BY. These commands are like tidying up a messy desk: sorting puts everything in a clear sequence, and grouping stacks similar items together for a bigger picture. I'm thrilled to guide you through this—it's where your data starts to look polished and purposeful. We'll explore both, try tons of examples, and make sure you're comfy organizing your database like a pro. Ready to straighten things out? Let's get cracking!

Let's start with our trusty "friends" table, set up as "CREATE TABLE friends (id INTEGER PRIMARY KEY, name TEXT, age INTEGER);" with data: "1 | Liam | 32," "2 | Kate | 26," "3 | Sean | 29," "4 | Clare | 23," "5 | Pat | 35." Check it with "SELECT * FROM friends;" in your terminal (at "sqlite>") or DB Browser's "Browse Data" tab. If it's not there, recreate it and INSERT those rows—your starting point's set!

Sorting with ORDER BY

ORDER BY sorts your results—think of it as arranging a list alphabetically or numerically. Try "SELECT name, age FROM friends ORDER BY age;"—you'll see "Clare | 23," "Kate | 26," "Sean | 29," "Liam | 32," "Pat | 35." It's youngest to oldest—default is ascending (low to high). Run it in DB Browser's "Execute SQL" (hit F5) or terminal—rows line up nicely. Reverse it with DESC: "SELECT name, age FROM friends ORDER BY age DESC;"—"Pat | 35," "Liam | 32," "Sean | 29," "Kate | 26," "Clare | 23"—oldest first.

Sort by names: "SELECT name, age FROM friends ORDER BY name;"—"Clare | 23," "Kate | 26," "Liam | 32," "Pat | 35," "Sean | 29"—alphabetical, A to Z. "SELECT * FROM friends ORDER BY name DESC;"—"Sean | 29," "Pat | 35," "Liam | 32," "Kate | 26,"

"Clare | 23"—Z to A, full rows. Multiple columns? "SELECT name, age FROM friends ORDER BY age, name;"—if ages tie, names sort: "Clare | 23," "Kate | 26," "Sean | 29," "Liam | 32," "Pat | 35"—age first, then name within ties (none here, but it's ready).

Add cities: "ALTER TABLE friends ADD COLUMN city TEXT; UPDATE friends SET city = 'Galway' WHERE id IN (1, 3); UPDATE friends SET city = 'Dublin' WHERE id IN (2, 4); UPDATE friends SET city = 'Cork' WHERE id = 5;." "SELECT name, city FROM friends ORDER BY city;"—"Cork | Pat," "Dublin | Clare," "Dublin | Kate," "Galway | Liam," "Galway | Sean"—cities A to Z, NULLs last (if any). "SELECT name, city FROM friends ORDER BY city DESC, name;"—"Galway | Sean," "Galway | Liam," "Dublin | Kate," "Dublin | Clare," "Cork | Pat"—cities Z to A, names A to Z within.

Filter first: "SELECT name, age FROM friends WHERE age > 25 ORDER BY age;"—"Kate | 26," "Sean | 29," "Liam | 32," "Pat | 35." "SELECT name, city FROM friends WHERE city LIKE '%n' ORDER BY name DESC;"—"Sean | Galway," "Kate | Dublin"—only Galway and Dublin end in "n." ORDER BY comes last—WHERE filters, then it sorts.

Grouping with GROUP BY

GROUP BY clumps rows by a column, perfect with aggregates (COUNT, SUM, etc.). "SELECT city, COUNT(*) AS friend_count FROM friends GROUP BY city;"—"Cork | 1," "Dublin | 2," "Galway | 2"—how many friends per city. "SELECT city, AVG(age) AS avg_age FROM friends GROUP BY city;"—"Cork | 35.0," "Dublin | 24.5," "Galway | 30.5"—average age per city. "SELECT city, SUM(age) AS total_age FROM friends GROUP BY city;"—"Cork | 35," "Dublin | 49," "Galway | 61."

Filter before grouping: "SELECT city, COUNT() AS over_25 FROM friends WHERE age > 25 GROUP BY city;"—"Cork | 1," "Dublin | 1," "Galway | 2"—Kate (26), Sean (29), Liam (32), Pat (35). Add ages:

"INSERT INTO friends (name, age, city) VALUES ('Aoife', 27, 'Dublin'), ('Mark', 28, 'Galway');"—now "SELECT city, COUNT() AS friend_count FROM friends GROUP BY city;"—"Cork | 1," "Dublin | 3," "Galway | 3."

Combine with ORDER BY: "SELECT city, COUNT(*) AS friend_count FROM friends GROUP BY city ORDER BY friend_count DESC;"—"Dublin | 3," "Galway | 3," "Cork | 1"—most friends first (Dublin and Galway tie, order varies). "SELECT city, AVG(age) AS avg_age FROM friends GROUP BY city ORDER BY avg_age;"—"Dublin | 25.3333," "Galway | 29.6667," "Cork | 35.0." Round it: "SELECT city, ROUND(AVG(age), 1) AS avg_age FROM friends GROUP BY city ORDER BY avg_age DESC;"—"Cork | 35.0," "Galway | 29.7," "Dublin | 25.3."

Practical Scenarios

Expenses: "CREATE TABLE expenses (id INTEGER PRIMARY KEY, item TEXT, cost REAL, category TEXT); INSERT INTO expenses VALUES (1, 'Rent', 500.50, 'Home'), (2, 'Food', 75.25, 'Daily'), (3, 'Bus', 20.00, 'Daily'), (4, 'Lights', 40.75, 'Home');." Sort: "SELECT item, cost FROM expenses ORDER BY cost DESC;"— "Rent | 500.50," "Food | 75.25," "Lights | 40.75," "Bus | 20.00." Group: "SELECT category, SUM(cost) AS total FROM expenses GROUP BY category;"—"Daily | 95.25," "Home | 541.25." "SELECT category, COUNT(*) AS items FROM expenses GROUP BY category ORDER BY items DESC;"—"Daily | 2," "Home | 2" (ties again).

Trips: "CREATE TABLE trips (id INTEGER PRIMARY KEY, destination TEXT, friend_id INTEGER); INSERT INTO trips VALUES (1, 'Paris', 1), (2, 'London', 2), (3, 'Rome', 4), (4, 'Paris', 3);." "SELECT destination, COUNT(*) AS trips FROM trips GROUP BY destination;"—"London | 1," "Paris | 2," "Rome | 1." "SELECT destination FROM trips ORDER BY destination;"—"London,"

"Paris," "Paris," "Rome." With friends: "SELECT friends.name, COUNT(trips.id) AS trip_count FROM friends LEFT JOIN trips ON friends.id = trips.friend_id GROUP BY friends.name ORDER BY trip_count DESC;"—"Liam | 1," "Sean | 1," "Clare | 1," "Kate | 1," "Pat | 0," "Aoife | 0," "Mark | 0."

Books: "CREATE TABLE books (id INTEGER PRIMARY KEY, title TEXT, reader_id INTEGER, pages INTEGER); INSERT INTO books VALUES (1, 'Dune', 1, 412), (2, '1984', 2, 328), (3, 'Hobbit', 1, 310), (4, 'Dracula', 3, 418);." "SELECT reader_id, SUM(pages) AS total_pages FROM books GROUP BY reader_id ORDER BY total_pages DESC;"—"1 | 722," "3 | 418," "2 | 328." Join: "SELECT friends.name, COUNT(books.id) AS book_count FROM friends LEFT JOIN books ON friends.id = books.reader_id GROUP BY friends.name ORDER BY book_count DESC, name;"—"Liam | 2," "Kate | 1," "Sean | 1," "Aoife | 0," etc.

Sales: "CREATE TABLE sales (sale_id INTEGER PRIMARY KEY, item_id INTEGER, quantity INTEGER, date TEXT); INSERT INTO sales VALUES (1, 1, 5, '2025-04-06'), (2, 1, 10, '2025-04-07'), (3, 2, 8, '2025-04-06'); CREATE TABLE items (item_id INTEGER PRIMARY KEY, item_name TEXT); INSERT INTO items VALUES (1, 'Bread'), (2, 'Milk');." "SELECT items.item_name, SUM(sales.quantity) AS total_sold FROM items LEFT JOIN sales ON items.item_id = sales.item_id GROUP BY items.item_name ORDER BY total_sold DESC;"—"Bread | 15," "Milk | 8." "SELECT date, COUNT(*) AS sales FROM sales GROUP BY date ORDER BY date;"—"2025-04-06 | 2," "2025-04-07 | 1."

Advanced Sorting and Grouping

Sort by expression: "SELECT name, age FROM friends ORDER BY age % 2, age;"—evens first (none here), then odds: "Clare | 23," "Kate | 26," "Sean | 29," "Liam | 32," "Pat | 35" (all odd). Group with HAVING (filters groups): "SELECT city, COUNT(*) AS friend_count

FROM friends GROUP BY city HAVING friend_count > 2;"—"Dublin | 3," "Galway | 3." "SELECT city, AVG(age) AS avg_age FROM friends GROUP BY city HAVING avg_age < 30 ORDER BY avg_age;"—"Dublin | 25.3."

Multi-column grouping: "ALTER TABLE friends ADD COLUMN status TEXT; UPDATE friends SET status = 'Active' WHERE id IN (1, 2, 3); UPDATE friends SET status = 'Inactive' WHERE id IN (4, 5, 6, 7);." "SELECT city, status, COUNT(*) AS count FROM friends GROUP BY city, status ORDER BY count DESC;"—"Dublin | Inactive | 2," "Galway | Active | 2," "Dublin | Active | 1," "Cork | Inactive | 1."

Troubleshooting

No sort? "SELECT name FROM friends ORDER BY ages;"—"no such column: ages"—fix to "age." Wrong order? "SELECT name FROM friends ORDER BY city;"—NULLs last, use "ORDER BY city IS NULL, city" for NULLs first. GROUP BY error? "SELECT name, COUNT() FROM friends;"—"must group by name too"—add it. Empty groups? "SELECT city, COUNT() FROM friends WHERE age > 40 GROUP BY city;"—no matches. Check "SELECT * FROM"—then organize. You're a sorting and grouping wizard—brilliant work!

Indexes: Speeding Up Your Searches

Welcome to the world of indexes—a secret weapon for making your database searches lightning-fast! If you've ever flipped through a book's index to find a topic quickly, you've got the gist of what we're doing here. In SQL, indexes are like shortcuts that help your database zip through rows instead of slogging through every single one. I'm excited to show you how they work—it's a bit like tuning up a bicycle to glide down Galway's hills with ease. We'll dig into creating, using, and managing indexes, with plenty of examples to try, so you can feel the difference they make. Don't worry if it sounds technical—I'll keep it simple and fun, and by the end, you'll be speeding up your searches like a pro. Ready to give your database a boost? Let's roll!

Let's start with our "friends" table, set up as "CREATE TABLE friends (id INTEGER PRIMARY KEY, name TEXT, age INTEGER);" with some data: "1 | Liam | 32," "2 | Kate | 26," "3 | Sean | 29," "4 | Clare | 23," "5 | Pat | 35." Check it with "SELECT * FROM friends;" in your terminal (at "sqlite>") or DB Browser's "Browse Data" tab. If it's not there, recreate it and INSERT those rows—your base is ready! With just five rows, speed's not an issue yet, but imagine hundreds or thousands—indexes shine there, and we'll scale up soon.

What's an Index?

An index is a special structure SQLite builds to track a column's values, like a book's index listing page numbers. Without it, a query like "SELECT * FROM friends WHERE age = 29;" scans every row—slow with big tables. An index on "age" acts like a cheat sheet, pointing straight to Sean's row. SQLite's PRIMARY KEY (id here) gets an index automatically—try "SELECT * FROM friends WHERE id = 3;"—it's fast already. But for other columns, you add indexes yourself.

Creating an Index

Let's index "age": "CREATE INDEX idx_age ON friends(age);"—no output, but it's done. "idx_age" is the name (pick anything clear), "friends" is the table, "age" the column. Check it in terminal: ".indices friends"—"idx_age" (and a hidden id index) shows up. In DB Browser, "Database Structure" tab lists "idx_age" under "Indexes." Test it: "SELECT * FROM friends WHERE age = 29;"—"3 | Sean | 29." With five rows, you won't feel the speed yet, but trust me—it's primed!

Add more: "INSERT INTO friends (name, age) VALUES ('Aoife', 27), ('Mark', 28), ('Ellen', 24), ('John', 33), ('Clare', 23);"—10 rows now. "SELECT * FROM friends WHERE age = 23;"—"4 | Clare | 23," "10 | Clare | 23"—index helps, especially as data grows. Multi-column index: "CREATE INDEX idx_name_age ON friends(name, age);"—for queries like "SELECT * FROM friends WHERE name = 'Clare' AND age = 23;"—both Clares, faster.

Seeing the Difference

With 10 rows, speed's subtle, so let's scale up. Drop "friends": "DROP TABLE friends;"—recreate with more: "CREATE TABLE friends (id INTEGER PRIMARY KEY, name TEXT, age INTEGER);." Add 100 rows (manually or imagine a script): "INSERT INTO friends (name, age) VALUES ('Liam', 32), ('Kate', 26), ..., ('Friend99', 45);"—mix ages 20-50. Without an index, "SELECT * FROM friends WHERE age = 35;" scans all 100. "CREATE INDEX idx_age ON friends(age);"—rerun the query— SQLite jumps to matches (say, 5 friends aged 35) instantly. Real speed shows with thousands, but even here, it's smoother.

Unique Indexes

For unique data: "CREATE UNIQUE INDEX idx_name ON friends(name);"—no duplicate names allowed. "INSERT INTO friends (name, age) VALUES ('Liam', 40);"—"UNIQUE constraint failed"—Liam's already there. Drop it: "DROP INDEX idx_name;"—then "INSERT INTO friends (name, age) VALUES ('Liam', 40);"—works now, two Liams. Unique indexes enforce rules and speed searches.

Practical Scenarios

Expenses: "CREATE TABLE expenses (id INTEGER PRIMARY KEY, item TEXT, cost REAL, date TEXT); INSERT INTO expenses VALUES (1, 'Rent', 500.50, '2025-04-01'), (2, 'Food', 75.25, '2025-04-02'), (3, 'Bus', 20.00, '2025-04-02'), (4, 'Lights', 40.75, '2025-04-03');." "SELECT * FROM expenses WHERE date = '2025-04-02';"—Food and Bus. "CREATE INDEX idx_date ON expenses(date);"—rerun—faster, especially with more dates. "CREATE INDEX idx_cost ON expenses(cost);"—"SELECT * FROM expenses WHERE cost < 50.00 ORDER BY cost;"—Bus and Lights, quick and sorted.

Trips: "CREATE TABLE trips (id INTEGER PRIMARY KEY, destination TEXT, friend_id INTEGER); INSERT INTO trips VALUES (1, 'Paris', 1), (2, 'London', 2), (3, 'Rome', 4), (4, 'Paris', 3);." "CREATE INDEX idx_destination ON trips(destination);"—"SELECT * FROM trips WHERE destination = 'Paris';"—two Parises, snappy. Join boost: "CREATE INDEX idx_friend_id ON trips(friend_id);"—"SELECT friends.name, trips.destination FROM friends JOIN trips ON friends.id = trips.friend_id WHERE trips.destination = 'Paris';"—Liam and Sean, optimized.

Sales: "CREATE TABLE sales (sale_id INTEGER PRIMARY KEY, item_id INTEGER, quantity INTEGER, date TEXT); INSERT INTO sales VALUES (1, 1, 5, '2025-04-06'), (2, 1, 10, '2025-04-07'), (3, 2, 8, '2025-04-06'); CREATE TABLE items (item_id INTEGER PRIMARY KEY, item_name TEXT); INSERT INTO items VALUES (1, 'Bread'), (2, 'Milk');." "CREATE INDEX idx_date ON sales(date);"—"SELECT date, SUM(quantity) FROM sales GROUP BY date;"—"2025-04-06 | 13," "2025-04-07 | 10," faster grouping. "CREATE INDEX idx_item_id ON sales(item_id);"—"SELECT items.item_name, SUM(sales.quantity) FROM items LEFT JOIN sales ON items.item_id = sales.item_id GROUP BY items.item_name;"—Bread and Milk totals, sped up.

Managing Indexes

List them: ".indices friends"—all indexes for "friends." Drop one: "DROP INDEX idx_age;"—"SELECT * FROM friends WHERE age = 29;"—still works, just slower with big data. Rebuild: "CREATE INDEX idx_age ON friends(age);." Too many indexes? They speed reads but slow INSERT/UPDATE—each change updates indexes. "INSERT INTO friends (name, age) VALUES ('Test', 30);"—with five indexes, it's a tad slower than with one. Drop unneeded: "DROP INDEX idx_name_age;"—if rarely used.

Advanced Indexing

Partial index: "CREATE INDEX idx_young ON friends(age) WHERE age < 30;"—only indexes ages under 30. "SELECT * FROM friends WHERE age < 30;"—Kate, Clare, etc., fast; "SELECT * FROM friends WHERE age = 35;"—ignores index, full scan. Multi-column: "CREATE INDEX idx_city_age ON friends(city, age);"—"SELECT * FROM friends WHERE city = 'Galway' AND age > 30;"—Liam, quick.

Covering index (SQLite optimizes internally): "CREATE INDEX idx_name_city ON friends(name, city);"—"SELECT name, city FROM friends WHERE name = 'Liam';"—fetches from index, not table—super fast with big data. Check usage: "EXPLAIN QUERY PLAN SELECT * FROM friends WHERE age = 29;"—post-index, it says "USING INDEX idx_age"—proof it's working! Pre-index, it's "SCAN TABLE."

Troubleshooting

No speed-up? "SELECT * FROM friends WHERE age > 25;"—index on "age" helps equals (=), less ranges—try "= 29." Wrong column? "CREATE INDEX idx_name ON friends(name);"—"SELECT * FROM friends WHERE age = 30;"—no help, index "age" instead. ".indices" empty? Recreate lost indexes. Slow inserts? Too many indexes—drop extras. "SELECT * FROM" small tables—indexes shine with scale.

Real-World Boosts

Library: "CREATE TABLE books (id INTEGER PRIMARY KEY, title TEXT, author TEXT, reader_id INTEGER); INSERT INTO books VALUES (1, 'Dune', 'Herbert', 1), (2, '1984', 'Orwell', 2), (3, 'Hobbit', 'Tolkien', 1);." "CREATE INDEX idx_author ON books(author);"—"SELECT * FROM books WHERE author = 'Tolkien';"—Hobbit, fast.

Logs: "CREATE TABLE logs (log_id INTEGER PRIMARY KEY, date TEXT, action TEXT); INSERT INTO logs VALUES (1, '2025-04-06', 'Login'), (2, '2025-04-06', 'Logout'), (3, '2025-04-07', 'Login');." "CREATE INDEX idx_date ON logs(date);"—"SELECT COUNT(*) FROM logs WHERE date = '2025-04-06';"—2, quick.

Your searches are turbo-charged now—indexes make your database fly! Test with "SELECT * FROM"—then watch it soar. You're an indexing ace—fantastic work!

Building a Query Tool: Your Practical Data Finder

Alright, let's put your SQL skills to work and build something practical—a query tool! Imagine having a little system where you can quickly search your database for exactly what you need, like finding a friend by name or age, all with a few simple commands. This is your chance to turn those SELECT and WHERE skills into a hands-on tool you can use and tweak. I'm thrilled to guide you through this—it's like crafting a custom key to unlock your data, and I'll make sure it's clear and fun. We'll set it up in SQLite, using the terminal or DB Browser, with lots of examples to play with. By the end, you'll have a working finder you can show off, and I'll be right here cheering you on. Ready to build something useful? Let's get started!

We'll base this on our "friends" table, set up as "CREATE TABLE friends (id INTEGER PRIMARY KEY, name TEXT, age INTEGER);" with some starting data: "INSERT INTO friends (name, age) VALUES ('Liam', 32), ('Kate', 26), ('Sean', 29), ('Clare', 23), ('Pat', 35);." Check it with "SELECT * FROM friends;" in your terminal (at "sqlite>" after "sqlite3 mydb.db") or DB Browser's "Browse Data" tab—five rows, ids 1 to 5 auto-incremented. If it's not there, recreate it—your foundation's ready!

The Goal: A Simple Query Tool

Our tool will let you search "friends" by name or age, like asking, "Who's named Kate?" or "Who's 29?" We'll do this manually in SQLite—typing queries as needed—since we're sticking to pure SQL (no Python here). You'll save these as reusable commands, switching between them to find what you want. It's basic but practical, teaching you to organize and run queries like a pro.

Step 1: Basic Searches

Start in the terminal: "sqlite3 mydb.db." Search by name: "SELECT * FROM friends WHERE name = 'Kate';"—"2 | Kate | 26." By age: "SELECT * FROM friends WHERE age = 29;"—"3 | Sean | 29." In DB Browser, open "mydb.db," go to "Execute SQL," type those queries, and hit F5—results appear below. Simple, right? But typing each time's a chore—let's save them.

In DB Browser, write "SELECT * FROM friends WHERE name = 'Kate';" in "Execute SQL," click "Save As," name it "name_search.sql," and save in "MySQLProjects." For age: "SELECT * FROM friends WHERE age = 29;"—save as "age_search.sql." Reload by clicking "Open" and selecting the file, then F5—same results. In terminal, create files with a text editor (Notepad, TextEdit): "name_search.sql" with that name query, "age_search.sql" with the age one. Run them: ".read name_search.sql"—Kate; ".read age_search.sql"—Sean. Your tool's taking shape!

Step 2: Making It Flexible

Hardcoding 'Kate' or 29 limits us—let's generalize. In practice, you'd adjust the query each time. Add more friends: "INSERT INTO friends (name, age) VALUES ('Aoife', 27), ('Mark', 28), ('Ellen', 24);"—eight now. Terminal: "SELECT * FROM friends WHERE name = 'Aoife';"—"6 | Aoife | 27." Edit "name_search.sql" to "SELECT * FROM friends WHERE name = 'Aoife';"—".read name_search.sql"—Aoife again. For age: edit "age_search.sql" to "SELECT * FROM friends WHERE age = 28;"—".read age_search.sql"—"7 | Mark | 28." In DB Browser, update and resave those files—same process.

Multiple matches? "INSERT INTO friends (name, age) VALUES ('Clare', 23);"—two Clares. "SELECT * FROM friends WHERE name = 'Clare';"—"4 | Clare | 23," "9 | Clare | 23." Edit "name_search.sql" accordingly—run it, both show. "SELECT *

FROM friends WHERE age = 23;"—same two—update "age_search.sql" and test. Your tool handles duplicates!

Step 3: Expanding the Tool

Add a city column: "ALTER TABLE friends ADD COLUMN city TEXT; UPDATE friends SET city = 'Galway' WHERE id IN (1, 3, 7); UPDATE friends SET city = 'Dublin' WHERE id IN (2, 4, 6, 9); UPDATE friends SET city = 'Cork' WHERE id IN (5, 8);." "SELECT * FROM friends;"—ids 1-9, names, ages, cities. New query: "SELECT * FROM friends WHERE city = 'Galway';"—"1 | Liam | 32 | Galway," "3 | Sean | 29 | Galway," "7 | Mark | 28 | Galway." Save as "city_search.sql"—terminal: ".read city_search.sql"; DB Browser: load and run.

Mix it: "SELECT name, age FROM friends WHERE city = 'Dublin' AND age < 25;"—"4 | Clare | 23 | Dublin," "9 | Clare | 23 | Dublin." Save as "city_age_search.sql"—test it. Partial matches: "SELECT * FROM friends WHERE name LIKE '%e';"—Kate, Clare (x2), Aoife. Save as "name_pattern.sql"—run it. Your tool's versatile now— name, age, city, patterns!

Step 4: Organizing Your Queries

Create a folder, "QueryTool," in "MySQLProjects." Save all: "name_search.sql," "age_search.sql," "city_search.sql," "city_age_search.sql," "name_pattern.sql." In terminal, "cd MySQLProjects/QueryTool" then "sqlite3 ../../mydb.db"—path adjusts, ".read name_search.sql" works. In DB Browser, "Open" each from that folder—F5 runs them. Add notes in files: "-- Search by name" at the top of "name_search.sql"—edit the WHERE value each use.

More queries: "SELECT name, city FROM friends WHERE age BETWEEN 25 AND 30 ORDER BY age;"—"Kate | Dublin | 26," "Aoife | Dublin | 27," "Mark | Galway | 28," "Sean | Galway | 29."

Save as "age_range.sql." "SELECT COUNT(*) AS galway_count FROM friends WHERE city = 'Galway';"—"galway_count | 3"—save as "city_count.sql." Your collection's growing—pick and run as needed!

Practical Scenarios

Expenses: "CREATE TABLE expenses (id INTEGER PRIMARY KEY, item TEXT, cost REAL, date TEXT); INSERT INTO expenses VALUES (1, 'Rent', 500.50, '2025-04-01'), (2, 'Food', 75.25, '2025-04-02'), (3, 'Bus', 20.00, '2025-04-03');." "SELECT * FROM expenses WHERE date = '2025-04-02';"—"2 | Food | 75.25 | 2025-04-02"—save as "date_search.sql." "SELECT item, cost FROM expenses WHERE cost < 100;"—Bus and Food—save as "cost_search.sql." Run ".read date_search.sql" or load in DB Browser—your expense finder!

Trips: "CREATE TABLE trips (id INTEGER PRIMARY KEY, destination TEXT, friend_id INTEGER); INSERT INTO trips VALUES (1, 'Paris', 1), (2, 'London', 2), (3, 'Rome', 4);." "SELECT friends.name, trips.destination FROM friends JOIN trips ON friends.id = trips.friend_id WHERE destination = 'Paris';"—"Liam | Paris"—save as "dest_search.sql." "SELECT COUNT(*) AS trip_count FROM trips WHERE friend_id = 1;"—"trip_count | 1"—save as "friend_trip_count.sql." Your trip finder's live!

Books: "CREATE TABLE books (id INTEGER PRIMARY KEY, title TEXT, reader_id INTEGER); INSERT INTO books VALUES (1, 'Dune', 1), (2, '1984', 2);." "SELECT friends.name, books.title FROM friends JOIN books ON friends.id = books.reader_id WHERE title = 'Dune';"—"Liam | Dune"—save as "title_search.sql." "SELECT * FROM friends LEFT JOIN books ON friends.id = books.reader_id WHERE books.id IS NULL;"—non-readers—save as "no_books.sql." Book tool ready!

Step 5: Enhancing the Tool

Add indexes for speed: "CREATE INDEX idx_name ON friends(name);"—"SELECT * FROM friends WHERE name = 'Sean';" zips. "CREATE INDEX idx_city ON friends(city);"—"city_search.sql" flies. Test: "EXPLAIN QUERY PLAN SELECT * FROM friends WHERE city = 'Galway';"—"USING INDEX idx_city"—proof it's optimized.

Error handling: "SELECT * FROM friends WHERE name = 'Bob';"—empty, fine. Save "not_found.sql" with "SELECT 'No match found' AS message WHERE NOT EXISTS (SELECT 1 FROM friends WHERE name = 'Bob');"—"message | No match found" if Bob's absent. Edit per search—your tool warns you!

Formatting: "SELECT id || ': ' || name || ', Age: ' || age || ', City: ' || city AS friend_info FROM friends WHERE city = 'Dublin';"—"2: Kate, Age: 26, City: Dublin," etc.—save as "pretty_city_search.sql"—readable output.

Using Your Tool

Terminal workflow: "sqlite3 mydb.db," ".read city_search.sql"—edit file for new cities (e.g., 'Cork'). DB Browser: open "mydb.db," load "age_search.sql," tweak to 35, F5—Pat. Add data: "INSERT INTO friends (name, age, city) VALUES ('John', 33, 'Cork');"—rerun queries, updated results. Your tool adapts—search name, age, city, or mix!

Troubleshooting

No results? Check spelling—"SELECt" fails, fix to "SELECT." Wrong file? ".read name_search"—needs ".sql"—"path not found" if folder's off. Empty? "SELECT * FROM friends WHERE age = 50;"—no 50-year-olds. "SELECT * FROM"—confirm data, then tweak queries. DB Browser locked? Close terminal first—only one uses "mydb.db."

Your query tool's a gem—name_search.sql, age_search.sql, and more, all at your fingertips! Edit, run, explore—you're finding data like a pro. Fantastic work!

Your First Project: Building a Task Tracker

Welcome to your first proper SQL project—a task tracker! This is where all your skills come together to create something you can really use, like a digital to-do list that keeps track of what you need to do and what's done. Imagine jotting down tasks, checking them off, and seeing what's left—all stored neatly in a database. I'm chuffed to bits to guide you through this—it's like building a little helper for your day, and I'll make it clear and enjoyable. We'll set it up in SQLite, using the terminal or DB Browser, with loads of examples and tweaks to make it your own. By the end, you'll have a working tracker to show off, and I'll be right here cheering you on. Ready to get organized? Let's dive in!

We'll build this from scratch, starting with a fresh table. Open your terminal with "sqlite3 mydb.db" or load DB Browser with "mydb.db"—your workspace is set. If "mydb.db" has old tables, start a new one like "sqlite3 task_tracker.db" to keep it separate—your call!

Step 1: Setting Up the Task Table

Let's create the core: "CREATE TABLE tasks (id INTEGER PRIMARY KEY, task TEXT, done INTEGER);"—id auto-increments, task holds the description, done is 0 (not done) or 1 (done). Run it—no output means success. Check in terminal: ".tables"—"tasks" shows. In DB Browser, "Database Structure" lists "tasks." Add a task: "INSERT INTO tasks (task, done) VALUES ('Call mom', 0);"—"SELECT * FROM tasks;"—"1 | Call mom | 0." Your tracker's alive!

Add more: "INSERT INTO tasks (task, done) VALUES ('Buy bread', 0), ('Read book', 0);"—"SELECT * FROM tasks;"—three rows: "1 | Call mom | 0," "2 | Buy bread | 0," "3 | Read book | 0." Save as "add_task.sql" in a "TaskTracker" folder: "INSERT INTO tasks (task, done) VALUES ('New task', 0);"—edit 'New task' each time.

Terminal: ".read add_task.sql" (after "cd TaskTracker"); DB Browser: load and run—your add function's set!

Step 2: Viewing Tasks

See what's pending: "SELECT id, task, done FROM tasks WHERE done = 0;"—all three show. Save as "view_pending.sql"—run it: ".read view_pending.sql" or F5 in DB Browser. All tasks: "SELECT id, task, done FROM tasks;"—save as "view_all.sql." Pretty it up: "SELECT id || ': ' || task || ' - ' || CASE WHEN done = 0 THEN 'Not Done' ELSE 'Done' END AS task_info FROM tasks;"—"1: Call mom - Not Done," etc.—save as "view_pretty.sql." CASE turns 0/1 into words—your list looks sharp!

Filter by id: "SELECT * FROM tasks WHERE id = 2;"—"2 | Buy bread | 0"—save as "view_by_id.sql," edit id as needed. Count pending: "SELECT COUNT(*) AS pending FROM tasks WHERE done = 0;"—"pending | 3"—save as "count_pending.sql." Your view options are growing—pick what you need!

Step 3: Marking Tasks Done

Mark "Call mom" done: "UPDATE tasks SET done = 1 WHERE id = 1;"—"SELECT * FROM tasks WHERE id = 1;"—"1 | Call mom | 1." Save as "mark_done.sql": "UPDATE tasks SET done = 1 WHERE id = [number];"—replace [number] each time (e.g., 2). Run ".read mark_done.sql" or edit in DB Browser—test with "2": "2 | Buy bread | 1." "SELECT * FROM tasks;"—two done, one not. Undo: "UPDATE tasks SET done = 0 WHERE id = 2;"—flexible!

Bulk mark: "UPDATE tasks SET done = 1 WHERE task LIKE '%bread';"—bread's done. Save as "mark_by_task.sql"—edit the pattern. "SELECT * FROM tasks WHERE done = 1;"—done tasks only—save as "view_done.sql." Your tracker's checking off like a champ!

Step 4: Enhancing the Tracker

Add dates: "ALTER TABLE tasks ADD COLUMN due_date TEXT;"—update: "UPDATE tasks SET due_date = '2025-04-07' WHERE id = 1; UPDATE tasks SET due_date = '2025-04-08' WHERE id = 2; UPDATE tasks SET due_date = '2025-04-09' WHERE id = 3;." "SELECT * FROM tasks;"—ids, tasks, done, due_dates. New add: "INSERT INTO tasks (task, done, due_date) VALUES ('Email boss', 0, '2025-04-10');"—save as "add_with_date.sql."

View by date: "SELECT id, task, due_date FROM tasks WHERE due_date = '2025-04-08';"—"2 | Buy bread | 2025-04-08"—save as "view_by_date.sql." Overdue: "SELECT id, task, due_date FROM tasks WHERE due_date < '2025-04-09' AND done = 0;"—assuming today's 2025-04-06, "Call mom" and "Buy bread" if not done—save as "view_overdue.sql." Sort: "SELECT task, due_date FROM tasks ORDER BY due_date;"—save as "view_sorted.sql."

Priorities: "ALTER TABLE tasks ADD COLUMN priority INTEGER DEFAULT 1;"—1 low, 3 high. "UPDATE tasks SET priority = 3 WHERE id = 1; UPDATE tasks SET priority = 2 WHERE id = 4;." "SELECT task, priority FROM tasks ORDER BY priority DESC;"— "Call mom | 3," "Email boss | 2," etc.—save as "view_by_priority.sql." Add with priority: "INSERT INTO tasks (task, done, priority) VALUES ('Fix bike', 0, 2);"—update "add_with_date.sql" to "INSERT INTO tasks (task, done, due_date, priority) VALUES ('New task', 0, 'YYYY-MM-DD', 1);."

Step 5: Practical Scenarios

Work tasks: "INSERT INTO tasks (task, done, due_date, priority) VALUES ('Finish report', 0, '2025-04-07', 3), ('Team meeting', 0, '2025-04-08', 2);." "SELECT task, due_date FROM tasks WHERE priority > 1 ORDER BY due_date;"—"Finish report | 2025-04-07," etc.—save as "view_urgent.sql." Mark: "UPDATE tasks SET done = 1 WHERE task = 'Team meeting';"—check "view_done.sql."

Home chores: "INSERT INTO tasks (task, done) VALUES ('Wash dishes', 0), ('Vacuum', 0);." "SELECT COUNT(*) AS chores FROM tasks WHERE done = 0 AND due_date IS NULL;"—"chores | 2"—save as "count_chores.sql." "UPDATE tasks SET done = 1 WHERE task = 'Wash dishes';"—one left.

Shopping list: "ALTER TABLE tasks ADD COLUMN category TEXT; UPDATE tasks SET category = 'Shopping' WHERE task LIKE '%bread'; UPDATE tasks SET category = 'Work' WHERE priority > 1;." "SELECT task FROM tasks WHERE category = 'Shopping' AND done = 0;"—"Buy bread" if not done—save as "view_category.sql."

Step 6: Optimizing and Managing

Index for speed: "CREATE INDEX idx_due_date ON tasks(due_date);"—"SELECT * FROM tasks WHERE due_date = '2025-04-07';" zips. "CREATE INDEX idx_category ON tasks(category);"—"view_category.sql" flies. Check: ".indices tasks"—lists them. Drop: "DROP INDEX idx_due_date;"—if unused.

Clear done: "DELETE FROM tasks WHERE done = 1;"—"SELECT * FROM tasks;"—pending only—save as "clear_done.sql." Reset: "DELETE FROM tasks;"—start fresh—save as "reset.sql." Backup: copy "task_tracker.db" to "backup.db"—restore if needed.

Step 7: Using Your Tracker

Terminal: "sqlite3 task_tracker.db," ".read add_with_date.sql" (edit task/date/priority), ".read view_pending.sql"—see what's up. DB Browser: open "task_tracker.db," load "mark_done.sql" (edit id), F5—"view_pretty.sql" shows progress. Add: "INSERT INTO tasks (task, done, due_date, category) VALUES ('Call Aoife', 0, '2025-04-11', 'Personal');"—"view_by_date.sql" for '2025-04-11.' Mark done, check counts—your day's under control!

Troubleshooting

No tasks? "SELECT * FROM tasks WHERE id = 5;"—empty if not added—check "SELECT * FROM tasks;." Typo? "UPATE" fails—fix to "UPDATE." Wrong date? "2025-13-01"—invalid, use "2025-04-01." "no such table"—wrong db—use "sqlite3 task_tracker.db." Locked? Close other tools—one at a time.

Your task tracker's a beauty—add, view, mark, sort, all in SQL! Tweak those .sql files—your to-dos are tamed. You're a project-building star—brilliant work!

Troubleshooting: Solving Common Problems

Welcome to the troubleshooting corner—where we tackle the bumps you might hit while working with SQL! Don't worry if things go wonky; errors are just part of the learning journey, like spilling tea while brewing your first pot. I'm here to help you mop up the mess and get back on track with a smile. This section's all about spotting common problems, figuring out why they happen, and fixing them with clear, practical steps. We'll cover a heap of issues—typos, missing tables, empty results, and more—with examples galore so you can see how to sort them out. By the end, you'll be a pro at fixing hiccups, and I'll be right beside you, cheering you on. Ready to play detective with your database? Let's dive in!

We'll use our "friends" table as a base: "CREATE TABLE friends (id INTEGER PRIMARY KEY, name TEXT, age INTEGER);" with data like "1 | Liam | 32," "2 | Kate | 26," "3 | Sean | 29," "4 | Clare | 23," "5 | Pat | 35." Open your terminal with "sqlite3 mydb.db" or DB Browser with "mydb.db"—check "SELECT * FROM friends;" to confirm. If it's not there, recreate it—your sandbox is set!

"no such table" Error

You type "SELECT * FROM friends;"—"Error: no such table: friends." Why? The table's not created yet, or you're in a new database. Fix it: "CREATE TABLE friends (id INTEGER PRIMARY KEY, name TEXT, age INTEGER);"—then INSERT your data. Rerun—works now! In terminal, maybe "mydb.db" is fresh—check ".tables"—empty? Recreate. In DB Browser, "Database Structure" shows no "friends"—add it via "Create Table" or SQL. Wrong db? "sqlite3 wrong.db"—"SELECT * FROM friends;"—fails if "friends" is in "mydb.db." Switch: "sqlite3 mydb.db."

Scenario: You've got "tasks" from your tracker project in "task_tracker.db," but "sqlite3 mydb.db"—"SELECT * FROM tasks;"—"no such table." Open "task_tracker.db" instead—problem solved!

"syntax error near [something]"

"SELECt * FROM friends;"—"syntax error near 'SELECt'." SQL's picky—fix to "SELECT * FROM friends;"—works. "UPDATE friends SET age = 30 WERE id = 1;"—"syntax error near 'WERE'." Should be "WHERE"—"UPDATE friends SET age = 30 WHERE id = 1;"—Liam's 30. Missing semicolon? "SELECT * FROM friends"—fine in terminal, but DB Browser might grumble—add ";"—consistent now.

Complex case: "INSERT INTO friends (name age) VALUES ('John' 33);"—"syntax error near 'age'." Missing commas—"INSERT INTO friends (name, age) VALUES ('John', 33);"—fixed. Quotes matter: "INSERT INTO friends (name, age) VALUES (John, 33);"—"syntax error near 'John'"—add quotes around 'John.' "SELECT * FROM friends WHERE name LIKE %a;"—"syntax error near '%a'"—needs quotes: "SELECT * FROM friends WHERE name LIKE '%a';"—Clare, Kate.

"no such column"

"SELECT name, city FROM friends;"—"no such column: city." You haven't added it—check "PRAGMA table_info(friends);" (terminal) or "Database Structure"—id, name, age only. Fix: "ALTER TABLE friends ADD COLUMN city TEXT;"—then "UPDATE friends SET city = 'Galway' WHERE id = 1;"—"SELECT name, city FROM friends;"—Liam's got Galway, others NULL. Typo? "SELECT nmae FROM friends;"—"no such column: nmae"—correct to "name."

Join issue: "SELECT friends.name, trips.dest FROM friends JOIN trips ON friends.id = trips.friend_id;"—"no such column: trips.dest." Table exists, column doesn't—create "CREATE TABLE trips (id INTEGER PRIMARY KEY, destination TEXT, friend_id INTEGER);"—use "destination"—"SELECT friends.name, trips.destination FROM friends JOIN trips ON friends.id = trips.friend_id;"—works after INSERTs.

No Results Returned

"SELECT * FROM friends WHERE age = 50;"—nothing? Your data tops at 35—check "SELECT MAX(age) FROM friends;"—35. Adjust: "SELECT * FROM friends WHERE age = 29;"—Sean's there. "SELECT * FROM friends WHERE name = 'Bob';"—no Bob—confirm "SELECT name FROM friends;"—no match. Case? "SELECT * FROM friends WHERE name = 'liam';"—SQLite's case-insensitive, but "Liam" works too—still him.

Empty join: "SELECT friends.name, trips.destination FROM friends JOIN trips ON friends.id = trips.friend_id;"—nothing? "SELECT * FROM trips;"—empty—INSERT data: "INSERT INTO trips VALUES (1, 'Paris', 1);"—rerun—Liam's trip shows. "WHERE" too strict: "SELECT * FROM friends WHERE age > 25 AND city = 'Dublin';"—none yet—add "UPDATE friends SET city = 'Dublin' WHERE id = 2;"—Kate now.

"database is locked"

Terminal: "INSERT INTO friends (name, age) VALUES ('John', 33);"—"database is locked." DB Browser's open—SQLite allows one writer at a time. Close DB Browser, retry—works. Reverse case: DB Browser's "Execute SQL" fails—terminal's holding it. ".exit" in terminal—DB Browser's free. Fix: use one tool at a time or save, close, reopen "mydb.db."

"UNIQUE constraint failed"

"INSERT INTO friends (id, name, age) VALUES (1, 'John', 33);"— "UNIQUE constraint failed: friends.id." Id 1 (Liam) exists— PRIMARY KEY must be unique. Let it auto-increment: "INSERT INTO friends (name, age) VALUES ('John', 33);"—id 6 next. Or drop uniqueness: "DROP TABLE friends; CREATE TABLE friends (id INTEGER, name TEXT, age INTEGER);"—allows duplicates, but PRIMARY KEY's better.

"column count doesn't match value count"

"INSERT INTO friends VALUES (1, 'John');"—"column count doesn't match value count at row 1." Three columns (id, name, age), two values—fix: "INSERT INTO friends VALUES (1, 'John', 33);" or "INSERT INTO friends (id, name) VALUES (1, 'John');"—specify columns.

Slow Queries

"SELECT * FROM friends WHERE age = 26;"—slow with 1000s of rows? No index—check "EXPLAIN QUERY PLAN SELECT * FROM friends WHERE age = 26;"—"SCAN TABLE." Add "CREATE INDEX idx_age ON friends(age);"—rerun—"USING INDEX"—faster! "SELECT * FROM friends WHERE name LIKE '%n';"—index on "name" won't help—LIKE with leading % scans all.

Practical Scenarios

Tasks: "SELECT * FROM tasks WHERE due_date = '2025-04-07';"—"no such table: tasks." Wrong db—"sqlite3 task_tracker.db"—fixed. "UPDTE tasks SET done = 1 WHERE id = 1;"—"syntax error"—"UPDATE"—done.

Expenses: "SELECT costt FROM expenses;"—"no such column: costt"—"cost." "SELECT SUM(cost) FROM expenses WHERE date = '2025-04-01';"—NULL—INSERT data first: "INSERT INTO expenses (item, cost, date) VALUES ('Rent', 500.50, '2025-04-01');"—now 500.50.

Joins: "SELECT friends.name, books.title FROM friends JOIN books ON friends.id = books.reader_id;"—empty—check "SELECT * FROM books;"—none—INSERT: "INSERT INTO books VALUES (1, 'Dune', 1);"—Liam's reading.

General Tips

Stuck in terminal? "Ctrl+C" or ".exit"—frees you. Odd output? "SELECT * FROM friends WHERE age = 'thirty-two';"—numbers, not text—"32." Online help: "sqlite syntax error near WHERE"— Google it—forums like Stack Overflow explain. "PRAGMA table_info(friends);"—shows columns—verify structure. ".schema"—all tables and CREATE statements—your map!

Lost data? "DROP TABLE friends;"—gone—recreate and INSERT. Backup "mydb.db" to "mydb_backup.db" before big changes—copy file. Test small: "SELECT * FROM friends LIMIT 2;"—check before full queries.

Your SQL's humming now—errors are just puzzles, and you've got the tools to solve them! "SELECT * FROM"—your safety net— troubleshoot like a pro. Fantastic work!

Going Further: What to Learn Next

You've made it this far—brilliant work! You've got the basics of SQL under your belt, from creating tables to building a task tracker, and now you're ready to stretch your wings a bit further. This section's all about what comes next—new skills to explore, tools to try, and projects to tackle that'll take your database know-how to the next level. I'm excited to point you down some paths that'll keep you growing, whether you're dreaming of managing bigger data, diving into real-world systems, or just having fun with what you've learned. I'll keep it practical and approachable, with plenty of ideas to spark your curiosity. Let's see where you can go from here—ready to take the next step?

Exploring Other SQL Systems

SQLite's been our trusty companion—lightweight and perfect for starting out—but there's a whole world of database systems waiting. Try MySQL—it's free, widely used, and great for web projects. Download it from mysql.com, install it, and connect via "mysql -u root -p" in your terminal (set a password during setup). Create a database: "CREATE DATABASE my_tasks; USE my_tasks;"—then recreate your "tasks" table: "CREATE TABLE tasks (id INT AUTO_INCREMENT PRIMARY KEY, task VARCHAR(255), done TINYINT);." Insert: "INSERT INTO tasks (task, done) VALUES ('Call mom', 0);"—"SELECT * FROM tasks;"—same feel, new flavor! MySQL's stricter—TEXT becomes VARCHAR with a length—but it's a smooth shift.

PostgreSQL's another gem—robust and feature-rich. Get it from postgresql.org, install, and use "psql -U postgres" (default user). "CREATE DATABASE tasks; \c tasks;"—then "CREATE TABLE tasks (id SERIAL PRIMARY KEY, task TEXT, done BOOLEAN);"— "INSERT INTO tasks (task, done) VALUES ('Buy bread', FALSE);"—"SELECT * FROM tasks;." BOOLEAN (TRUE/FALSE) vs. SQLite's 0/1—fancy! Both scale better than SQLite for big data—try porting your tracker and feel the power.

Advanced SQL Features

Subqueries add depth: "SELECT name FROM friends WHERE age > (SELECT AVG(age) FROM friends);"—friends above average age (e.g., Liam, Pat if average is ~29). Nested: "SELECT task FROM tasks WHERE due_date = (SELECT MIN(due_date) FROM tasks WHERE done = 0);"—earliest undone task. Save as "next_task.sql"—your tracker's smarter!

Constraints keep data tight: Recreate "friends" as "CREATE TABLE friends (id INTEGER PRIMARY KEY, name TEXT NOT NULL, age INTEGER CHECK (age > 0));"—no blank names or negative ages. "INSERT INTO friends (name, age) VALUES (NULL, 25);"—"NOT NULL constraint failed." "INSERT INTO friends (name, age) VALUES ('John', -5);"—"CHECK constraint failed." Foreign keys link tables: "CREATE TABLE trips (id INTEGER PRIMARY KEY, destination TEXT, friend_id INTEGER, FOREIGN KEY (friend_id) REFERENCES friends(id));"—no trips for non-existent friends. "INSERT INTO trips VALUES (1, 'Paris', 999);"—fails unless friend 999 exists—data stays connected!

Views save queries: "CREATE VIEW pending_tasks AS SELECT task, due_date FROM tasks WHERE done = 0;"—"SELECT * FROM pending_tasks;"—instant pending list. "DROP VIEW pending_tasks;"—if unneeded. Triggers automate: "CREATE TRIGGER mark_done_date AFTER UPDATE OF done ON tasks WHEN NEW.done = 1 BEGIN UPDATE tasks SET due_date = 'Done: ' || date('now') WHERE id = NEW.id; END;"—marking done adds today's date (e.g., "Done: 2025-04-06"). Test: "UPDATE tasks SET done = 1 WHERE id = 1;"—check it!

New Projects to Try

Build a budget tracker: "CREATE TABLE budget (id INTEGER PRIMARY KEY, item TEXT, cost REAL, category TEXT, date TEXT);"—"INSERT INTO budget VALUES (1, 'Rent', 500.50, 'Home', '2025-04-01');"—"SELECT category, SUM(cost) AS total FROM budget GROUP BY category;"—track spending by type. Add "SELECT * FROM budget WHERE date LIKE '2025-04%' ORDER BY cost DESC;"—monthly view—save as "monthly_budget.sql."

Shop inventory: "CREATE TABLE inventory (item_id INTEGER PRIMARY KEY, item_name TEXT, quantity INTEGER, price REAL);"—"INSERT INTO inventory VALUES (1, 'Bread', 50, 2.50);"—"SELECT item_name, quantity * price AS value FROM inventory ORDER BY value DESC;"—stock worth. "UPDATE inventory SET quantity = quantity - 5 WHERE item_name = 'Bread';"—sales—save as "sell_item.sql."

Personal library: "CREATE TABLE books (id INTEGER PRIMARY KEY, title TEXT, author TEXT, read INTEGER DEFAULT 0);"—"INSERT INTO books VALUES (1, 'Dune', 'Herbert', 0);"—"SELECT title, author FROM books WHERE read = 0 ORDER BY author;"—to-read list—save as "unread_books.sql." "CREATE INDEX idx_author ON books(author);"—faster searches!

Learning Resources

Hit w3schools.com—its SQL tutorial covers subqueries, joins, and more with interactive examples. Try "SELECT * FROM Customers WHERE Country = 'Ireland';"—play in their sandbox. Coursera's "SQL for Data Science" (University of California) dives into analysis—great for number-crunching. Books? "SQL in 10 Minutes, Sams Teach Yourself" by Ben Forta—quick lessons for busy days. SQLite's docs (sqlite.org)—dry but gold for commands like "CREATE TRIGGER."

Online communities: Stack Overflow—search "sqlite unique constraint failed"—tons of fixes. Reddit's r/SQL—post "How do I speed up this query?"—friendly folks reply. YouTube? "SQL Tutorial for Beginners" by freeCodeCamp—watch joins in action.

Mixing with Other Skills

Pair SQL with spreadsheets—export "SELECT * FROM tasks;" in DB Browser (File > Export > CSV)—open in Excel, filter, chart. Command line? "sqlite3 mydb.db 'SELECT * FROM friends;' > friends.txt"—data to file. Web dreams? Learn MySQL with PHP—simple pages showing "tasks." My other book, Learn Python: A Beginner's Guide to Coding with Ease, ties in—Python with SQLite (import sqlite3) automates queries—grab it if you fancy coding beyond SQL!

Keep experimenting—small projects grow skills. A review of this book'd help me heaps—let me know what clicked or didn't on Amazon or wherever you found it. You're on a roll—wherever you go next, you've got this!

About the Author: Liam Doherty

Here's a bit about me, Liam Doherty—the fella who's been guiding you through this SQL adventure. I hail from Galway, Ireland, a wild and wonderful spot on the western coast where the Atlantic breeze keeps things fresh and the craic's always mighty. In my late 30s now, I'm a red-haired coder with a quiet, curious streak, living in a cozy flat with my partner Aoife and our sly cat Síofra, who's likely napping on my keyboard as I type this. I've always loved teaching—spent years as a classroom teacher before tech stole my heart—and I get a real kick out of helping beginners like you find your footing in something new. This book's my way of sitting down with you over a cuppa, breaking SQL into friendly, manageable bits, and watching you shine as you get the hang of it.

My journey to SQL—and writing—came through a winding path. Back in Galway, I started tinkering with computers between lessons, drawn to how they could organize chaos into order. Teaching kids the basics of numbers and words sparked a love for explaining tricky stuff simply, and when I stumbled into coding, it clicked—databases like SQL were the perfect mix of structure and creativity. I've spent years since then guiding folks through data and code, from classroom chalk to online chats, always aiming to make it feel less like a chore and more like a chat by the fire. Living here, with the rugged coast just a stroll away, keeps me grounded—nothing beats a walk by the sea to clear the mind after a long coding session.

This isn't my first rodeo with a book—I also wrote Learn Python: A Beginner's Guide to Coding with Ease, a friendly dive into Python for folks starting out. It's been a hit with readers wanting to code their first programs, and if you've enjoyed this SQL journey, you might fancy giving it a whirl—Python and SQL pair up nicely for automating database tasks! I pour my heart into these guides, drawing on years of teaching and tech to make them clear and encouraging. When I'm not writing or coding, you'll find me brewing tea (strong, no sugar), digging into tech blogs, or wandering Galway's shores with Aoife, dreaming up the next project to share with you.

I'd love your thoughts on this book—writing's a bit like sending a message in a bottle, and hearing back means the world. If you've found it helpful, a quick review on Amazon, Goodreads, or wherever you grabbed it would be grand—tell me what worked, what didn't, or just say hi! It helps me tweak things for the next edition and lets others know if it's worth a read. I'm chuffed you've come along for this ride—here's to your next adventure, whatever it may be!

www.ingramcontent.com/pod-product-compliance
Lightning Source LLC
LaVergne TN
LVHW051615050326
832903LV00033B/4519